The Symmetry Wave Trading Method

THE SYMMETRY WAVE
TRADING METHOD

by Michael Gur

Windsor Books • Brightwaters, New York

Published by Windsor Books
P.O. Box 280
Brightwaters, N.Y. 11718

Manufactured in the United States of America

ISBN 0-930233-54-9

IMPORTANT NOTICE - PATENT PENDING

The technique for utilizing the Symmetry Wave concept, and underlying materials as disclosed herein, is the subject of a pending patent application. Such patent rights will be strictly enforced against violators.

CAVEAT: It should be noted that all commodity trades, patterns, charts, systems, etc., discussed in this book are for illustrative purposes only and are not to be construed as specific advisory recommendations. Further note that no method of trading or investing is foolproof or without difficulty, and past performance is no guarantee of future performance. All ideas and material presented are entirely those of the author and do not necessarily reflect those of the publisher or bookseller.

ACKNOWLEDGMENT

I thank Beloved who inspired me to do this work. I thank Phoebe Trimmer for doing editing and typing work often on an emergency basis. I also thank the editors at Windsor Books for their constant support in helping me to improve this book. Special thanks to my friends Otto A. Stark, Frank McLain, Susan Multon and Elizabeth St. Louis, for their positive outlook and support.

TABLE OF CONTENTS

FOREWORD

INTRODUCTION

FOREWORD

Trading the stock or futures markets is more complex than most traders realize. Trading is a vast perspective made up of chart interpretation, entry methods, exit methods, protective stops, money management, diversification, and psychology. Each of these subjects requires the development of a perspective. The total sum of these microperspectives make up the macroperspective that we call trading.

In this book, the Symmetry Wave Method is introduced as a means to organize a market and to rally around it all other elements of trading. Following is an outline to help you get a general idea of what's contained herein.

BROAD SUBJECT: Symmetry Wave Method™

WHAT IT DOES:
Organizes charts.
Analyzes markets.
Creates a new perspective.
Becomes a trading tool.
Singles out the major trend.

THE WAY IT WORKS:
Singles out waves.
Organizes waves into two categories
— trend waves and retracement waves.
Subdivides retracement waves.

THE GAP IT FILLS:
The first new method since the Elliott Wave Theory to organize markets; it removes many of the loopholes the Elliott Wave Theory cannot explain. The Symmetry Wave Method is a complete system which organizes and analyzes all markets; it is objective and goes far beyond idle, and often untradeable, theory.

OTHER TOOLS NECESSARY FOR SUCCESS:
The method of entry.
The method of exit.
The method of protecting a position.
Money management.
Diversification.
Psychology plays its part.

INTRODUCTION

There have been many books written on the stock and futures markets, trading methods, and analysis. Most of them are like an encyclopedia of various ideas and tools currently in use. Often someone comes along and repackages the same material under his/her own name. From my perspective, there has not been any viable new idea that realistically organizes and clarifies how markets work in fifty years. For example, when the Market Profile™ method of charting price fluctuations came onto the scene, many people went head over heels for it. An acquaintance of mine had attended a Market Profile™ seminar and was telling me that this was it and I should attend myself. At that time I was very involved analyzing five-minute bar charts of the Standard & Poor's 500 (as well as Treasury Bond charts). It took me just about a day to determine that Market Profile™ did not reveal anything more about market behavior than five-minute bar charts do. As had happened in my five-minute bar chart analysis, Market Profile™ found something that worked for a few months, only to be followed by a dismal trading period. In my mind that invalidated the Market Profile™ theory. A relatively recent craze has been candlestick charts. Here again, there is no consistent pattern which lasts long enough to be profitable.

You see, I've found that fundamental market behavior changes approximately every five months or so. This renders even a good mechanical system profitable for only a short time, followed by a non-profitable period and an overall flat performance. The reason for this is that indicators and charting techniques do not have intelligence or powers of discrimination. They merely mimic behavior up and down on horizontal axes; providing not much better than random chance for finding winning trades. Indicators do not and cannot distinguish between a sideways or trending market, nor do they provide a perspective as to how markets organize themselves.

The best a mechanical system can do is to provide a slight edge. That slight edge has proven ample enough for a number of capable stock and futures fund managers, providing — to the very best advisors — approximately a 20% average annualized return. For institutions, this is an excellent return on investment, making futures trading a viable investment field for banks, insurance companies, corporations and pension funds. In fact, managed money in the futures industry has grown in the past eight years from less than one billion dollars to well over twelve billion, with money pouring in at a rapid pace.

However, for many individual traders, having only a slight edge just doesn't cut it. Sweating out drawdowns that may last up to 18 months to achieve — if you're lucky — a five-year 20% annualized return is not only unacceptable, but for many, mentally not endurable. That's where Symmetry Wave enters the picture. It's a trading method capable of providing much more than "a slight edge" and targets returns substantially above those of the best funds.

Over the past 70 years there have been just a handful of original ideas that have gained respect in their attempts to organize and analyze markets and to increase knowledge as to how markets actually work. The most prominent approaches to date have come from W. D. Gann, the Dow Theory, and the Elliott Wave Theory. Each approach endeavored to organize the markets, yet for the vast majority of traders, these concepts remain untradeable in real-time. For example, it is now widely recognized that the Elliott Wave Theory is based on hindsight rather than foresight, obviously calling its tradeability into question.

The Symmetry Wave Method reveals what I consider to be the single most powerful way to first organize, then analyze, then profitably trade the markets. It provides a unique insight into price action and the overall structure of developing trends.

You will not find lengthy discussion and narrations in this book. The Symmetry Wave Method is presented in a direct and simple manner, accompanied by pertinent observations that have come from uncountable hours of research and trading, propelled by a passion to understand how markets organize themselves.

SECTION 1

Laying The Groundwork For The Symmetry Wave Trading Method

CHAPTER ONE

The Importance Of Having A Perspective

Whether it is someone who likes to establish a position in a market and keep it for several months, or someone who prefers to get in a market and exit within a few minutes, the framework of a perspective is essential for success. The object behind millions of hours of research by thousands of people has been to come up with a perspective through which they could earn money trading the markets. However, due to the complexity of the markets, it's been nearly impossible to come up with one successful perspective.

With the vast multitude of chart patterns, and varying magnitudes of price moves, it is unlikely that a single perspective can be found that will master all the possible complex patterns. For example, no single indicator can decipher between a slow-trending market, fast-trending market, and sideways market. Not even a combination of indicators can accomplish such a complex task. While it is possible to construct an indicator to take advantage of one specific pattern, that same indicator will perform miserably during incompatible patterns.

To emphasize how even a simple image can have several perspectives locked into it, here are a few illustrations. Each picture simultaneously contains two images or patterns. The first picture contains a rabbit and a duck, and the second picture contains a goblet and two faces looking at each other.

The following geometric pattern, a more complex image, can be seen as being made up of patterns arranged in different ways.

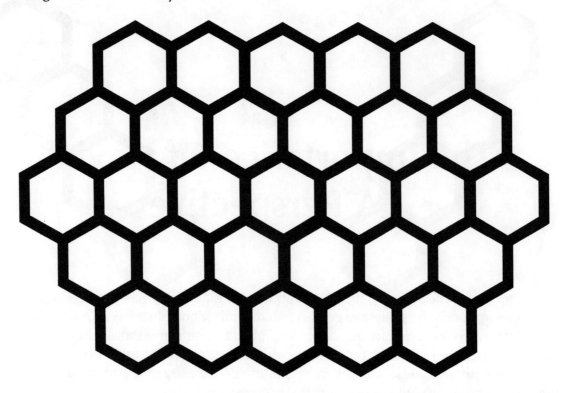

It is possible to see the above pattern as being made up of several flowerlike patterns, or . . .

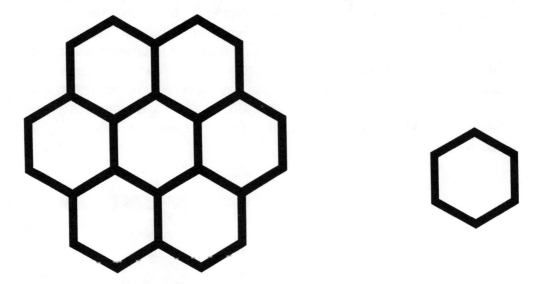

. . . it could be viewed as many hexagons arranged in horizontal rows, or . . .

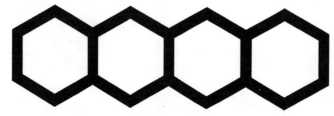

. . . it could be viewed as hexagons arranged in diagonal rows.

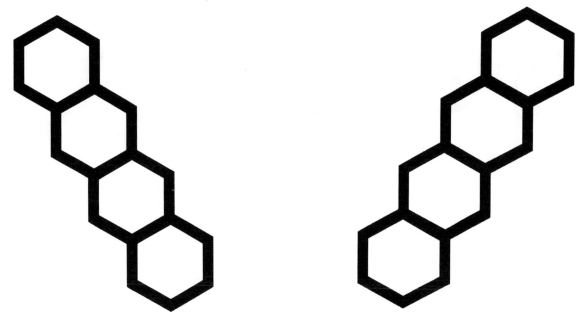

All of the above perspectives are correct, yet the mind can only focus on one pattern at a time.

You may have heard that trading is an art and not a science. Art is a subjective experience. If an art expert and you were to look at the same masterpiece, the art expert would see thoughts, feelings, imagery and perspective that you had not considered. This leads us to two very important observations. First, a chart is an image and contains many perspectives. Your perspective, or how you interpret a chart, will depend on your intentions. People interpret the same chart differently. Second, it is only possible to see one pattern or perspective at a time. Your mind may move very quickly between two perspectives but can only see one perspective at a time.

If you see two different possibilities as to how a market could progress, even if the difference is slight, it will lead to confusion and lack of confidence. Furthermore, since your attention and mind can only focus on one perspective at a time, in order to develop consistency and confidence, you should choose one of the following: to trade with or against the trend; to trade long-term or short-term; to trade a sideways market or a trending market. By switching between perspectives you can rationalize going both with and against a trend every trading day of the year. One idea, one perspective, one style of trading (plus consistency) lead to clarity and success. Compromise leads to confusion and confusion leads to chaos; therefore, it is necessary to choose a perspective to trade with, and ignore that which does not fit the perspective you have chosen.

In order to build a perspective, it is essential to reduce charts to their simpler components. A chart is a complex structure made up of price fluctuations. These price fluctuations are termed waves, and they come in many sizes. See Illustrations 1-1 and 1-2.

Later, in Chapter Three, we will demonstrate how organizing waves into the Symmetry Wave perspective helps make it easier to understand how markets function. Also, note in Illustration 1-2 that waves are made clearer by drawing lines through them.

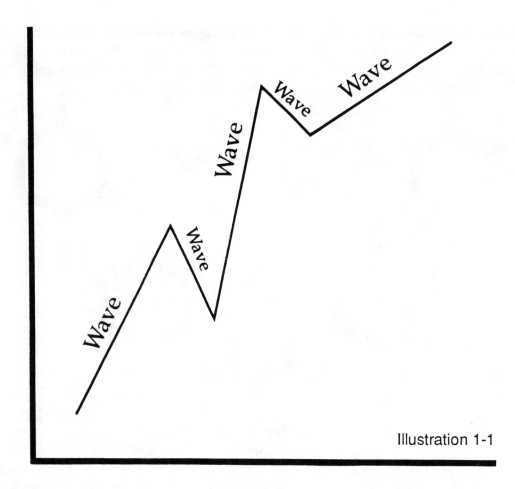

Illustration 1-1

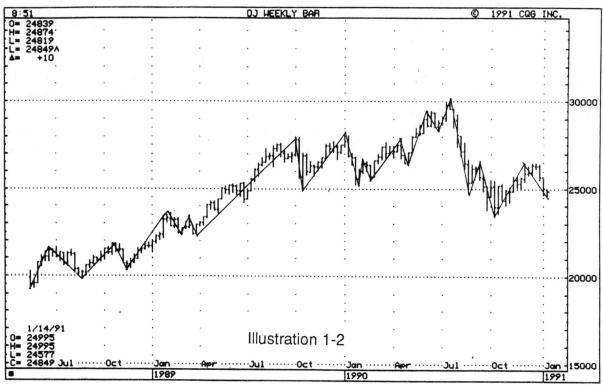

Illustration 1-2

The combination of small waves makes up a bigger wave (see Illustration 1-3) and a combination of all of the small and big waves makes a chart. To many readers, this is rudimentary; however, the awareness of the complex nature of waves will determine the proper organization of waves, entry price, protective stop, and profit targets.

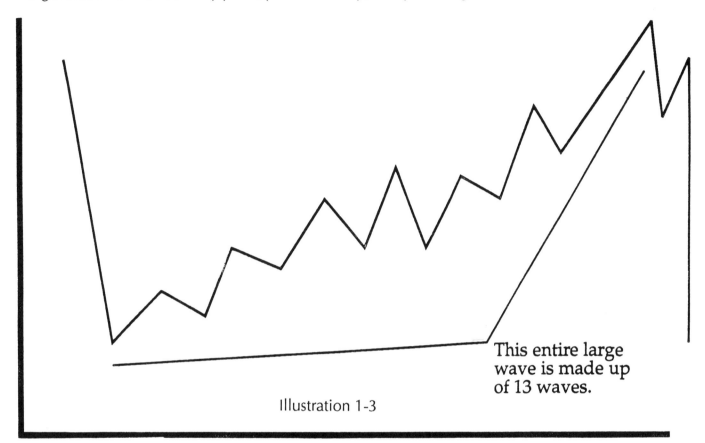

This entire large wave is made up of 13 waves.

Illustration 1-3

Each wave at a higher degree is a macrocosm that has a microcosm within it. What is a single wave at the monthly chart level is an entire chart at the daily level. In the same light, a single wave at the daily level is an entire chart at the fifteen-minute level. This progression continues down to a one-minute level. The last six bars on the monthly Dow Jones Industrial Index chart (Illustration 1-4), which is only one upwave, covers an entire chart made up of many complex waves at the daily Dow Jones Industrial Index level (Illustration 1-5). Illustration 1-6 is an S&P 500 chart made up of three-minute bars. This entire chart represents the complex price fluctuation of only one daily bar.

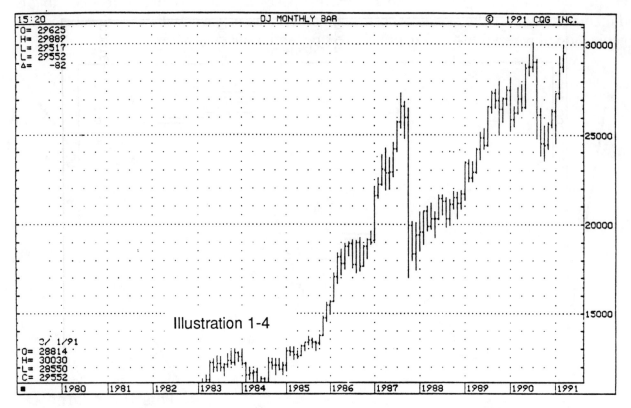

```
O= 29625
H= 29889
L= 29517
C= 29552
Δ=   -82
```

```
 3/1/91
O= 28814
H= 30030
L= 28550
C= 29552
```

Illustration 1-4

Dow Jones Industrial Index -- _INDU

Illustration 1-5

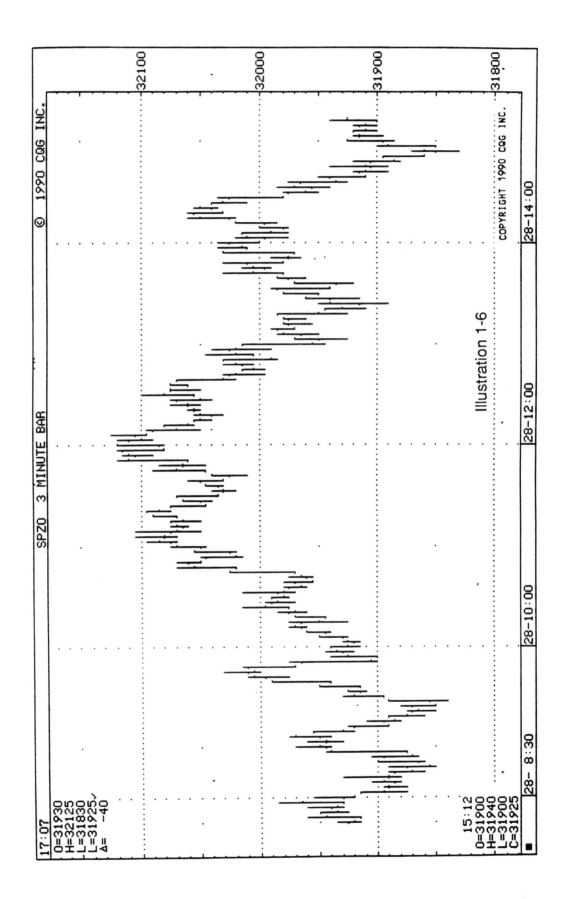

Illustration 1-6

As can be seen from the preceding examples, there would be too many waves to organize and to label if all price fluctuations were to be taken into account. Therefore, to organize the charts without having to count all price fluctuations, it pays to establish a minimum wave size that should be considered for possible wave count. To mathematically identify a wave size, we will use the ten-day average true range (ATR). ATR is defined as the greater of the following calculations.

    A. Today's high minus today's low.
    B. Today's high minus yesterday's close.
    C. Today's low minus yesterday's close.

On page nine is the tabular listing for the Gold chart which is in Illustration 1-7. The tabular listing starts from the cursor on the Gold chart which is on January 18, 1991. We will use these figures to illustrate how to calculate ATR for the past ten days. The absolute value is used in calculations because of the possible negative values.

At the closing of January 21, 1991, this is the calculation you would perform:

$$\text{High } \$383.9 \text{ minus low} \quad \$381.0 = \$2.9$$
$$\text{High } \$383.9 \text{ minus yesterday's close} \quad \$378.1 = \$5.8$$
$$\text{Low } \$381.0 \text{ minus yesterday's close} \quad \$378.1 = \$2.9$$

Since the largest true range (TR) is $5.8, this figure goes to the TR column. Then you add today's TR to the past nine days' TR. By dividing this total figure by ten, you get a ten-day ATR.

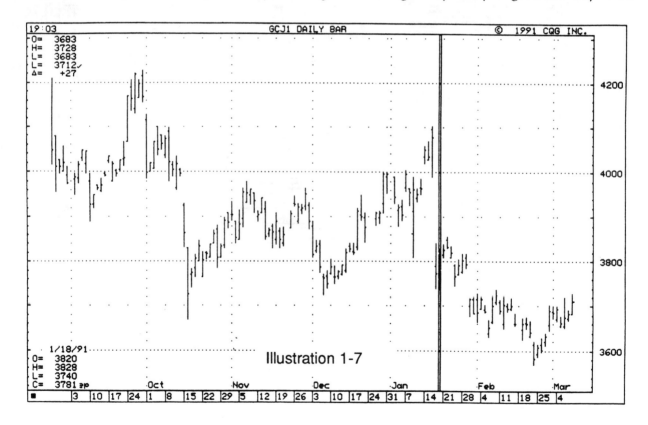

Illustration 1-7

Daily April Gold Prices for 1991 Futures

DATE	OPEN	HIGH	LOW	CLOSE	TR	Ten Day Total	Ten Day ATR
01/18/91	382.0	382.8	374.0	378.1			
01/21/91	381.5	383.9	381.0	382.6	$5.80		
01/22/91	385.0	385.5	383.0	383.3	2.90		
01/23/91	381.0	383.5	381.0	382.0	2.50		
01/24/91	379.3	379.5	374.5	376.6	7.50		
01/25/91	377.0	380.5	377.0	379.2	3.90		
01/28/91	377.8	381.7	377.5	380.2	4.20		
01/29/91	381.0	381.7	378.6	379.5	3.10		
01/30/91	370.0	371.7	367.8	371.5	11.70		
01/31/91	371.5	372.0	368.3	368.5	3.70		
02/01/91	371.5	372.8	366.5	368.7	6.30	$51.60	$5.16
02/04/91	369.5	372.0	369.5	371.6	3.30	49.10	4.91
02/05/91	369.3	370.4	368.7	368.9	2.90	49.10	4.91
02/06/91	364.0	367.0	363.0	365.2	5.90	52.50	5.25
02/07/91	366.5	372.4	366.2	370.0	7.20	52.20	5.22
02/08/91	371.0	373.7	370.6	372.4	3.70	52.00	5.20
02/11/91	370.9	371.3	368.5	369.1			
02/12/91	366.0	372.2	365.1	370.3			
02/13/91	370.0	370.8	368.8	369.5			
02/14/91	369.5	371.8	369.2	370.2			
02/15/91	366.0	368.5	365.6	366.1			
02/18/91	Holiday						
02/19/91	364.7	367.4	362.5	366.1			
02/20/91	366.3	367.6	365.0	366.1			
02/21/91	363.3	366.6	363.1	364.1			
02/22/91	361.3	362.0	357.0	368.3			
02/25/91	359.2	361.4	358.7	360.8			
02/26/91	361.3	362.9	359.7	360.2			
02/27/91	362.0	364.0	361.1	363.3			
02/28/91	365.8	370.3	364.5	369.0			
03/01/91	368.8	369.9	367.3	368.6			
03/04/91	367.2	370.0	366.7	369.5			
03/05/91	365.7	367.8	365.5	366.3			
03/06/91	365.7	372.0	365.2	367.5			
03/07/91	367.3	369.3	367.0	368.5			
03/08/91	368.3	372.8	368.3	371.2			

To further help us create a perspective and to interpret the charts, we will create four classifications of wave size. The definitions below are created, not so that one sticks to scientific interpretation of the above numbers but in order to have a common ground for communication. We will communicate more through illustration than the written word. Below are examples of different-sized waves. See Illustration 1-8.

- A.) 1.0 to 2.0 ATR is a miniwave.
- B.) 2.1 to 3.0 ATR is a small wave.
- C.) 3.1 to 4.0 ATR is a medium wave.
- D.) 4.1 and greater ATR is a big wave.

It is not our intention to calculate ATR all the time. It is not necessary. We are initially using ATR to mathematically illustrate wave sizes. Once the idea is grasped, then convert it to an art by visually seeing different-sized waves.

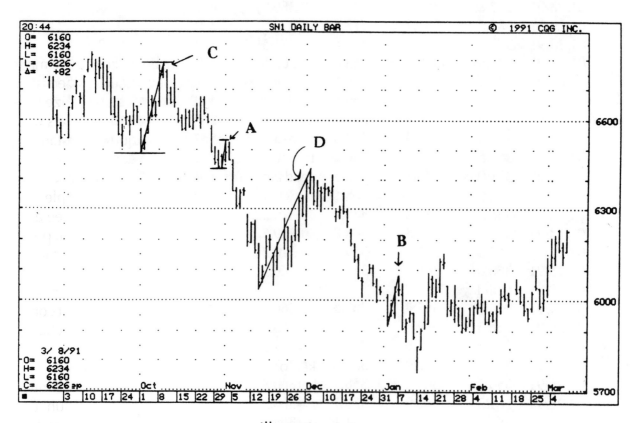

Illustration 1-8

Chapter Summary

One's knowledge, beliefs and intentions create a perspective. This perspective goes far to help or hinder one's ability to interpret or analyze a chart. By understanding how waves interact, it will be possible to organize the waves into a logical order.

CHAPTER TWO

Why The Elliott Wave Theory Does Not Work

Traders such as R. N. Elliott, W. D. Gann and Dr. L. Andrew, who are believed to have made millions of dollars trading the markets, acquired their unique perspectives after persistent analysis of the markets for many years. Subsequently, they developed tools to crystallize their perspectives (i.e., Elliott Wave Theory, Gann Lines and Andrews Meridian Line). Markets were their ruling passion, and each, after many years of research, acquired a unique understanding of market behavior. Therefore, to take their trading tools and to use them without their accompanying perspective of the markets often leads to frustration.

Simple proof that perspective has to precede any trading tool is in the fact that people who have used Gann Lines, the Andrews Meridian Line and the Elliott Wave Theory disagree as to the validity of these methods. We all have a different perception. Therefore what happens around a Gann Line, an Andrew Line or the Elliott Wave Theory is accordingly interpreted differently.

With experience comes what psychologists have termed the "ahaa" experience — a breakthrough in perception. Relating this to stock or futures charts, it is an experience that comes about when a chart makes greater sense. Creating a clearer understanding of market behavior is an objective of the Symmetry Wave Method.

Of all the tools available for analyzing a market, only the Symmetry Wave Method and the Elliott Wave Theory attempt to organize the markets. These two methods appear to be similar, yet they are drastically different in their objectivity and ability to organize a market, or to function as a trading tool. In this chapter the weaknesses of the Elliott Wave Theory will be explored. In Chapter 3, the Symmetry Wave Method will be explained in detail.

The Elliott Wave Theory states that a bull market fits into five wave patterns, three up and two intervening down waves. The five-wave-up pattern, then, is to be followed by a three-wave-down pattern. Therefore, the entire pattern is an eight-wave cycle (see Illustration 2-1).

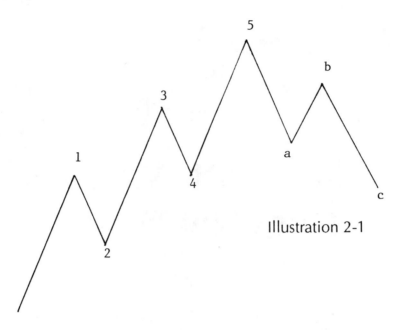

Illustration 2-1

The weakness of the Elliott Wave Theory lies in its rigid rule of five up waves and three down waves. Due to the fact that markets have their own agendas and more often than not refuse to fit the five-up-and-three-down rule, the Elliott Wave Theory has complex rules. This complexity causes inconsistency in wave count, hindsight adjustments, matching of unrelated magnitudes of waves, and complex wave extension. This is a problem of trying to fit a market into the Elliott Wave Theory.

There is no God-given rule that says a market has to develop in five waves and the correction has to be in three waves. When expectations are set the tendency is to ignore a wave, or to group a wave so as to make the wave count fit one's expectation.

Because the Elliott Wave Theory has major inadequacies, four specific weaknesses manifest themselves in real time trading.

1. Wave counts are complex and the variations of a wave count abound, leaving a trader with lack of confidence.
2. Just as indicators can be curve-fit to price data based on hindsight, so can the Elliott Wave Counts be curve-fit to charts based on hindsight.
3. Of itself, the Elliott Wave Theory does not anticipate support and resistance prices. Therefore, it is not a trading tool in and of itself but a fair tool for organizing a market.
4. Waves are skipped to make the market fit the Elliott Wave Theory.

Several illustrations follow to reinforce the above observations.

The Elliott wave count of the Dow Jones Industrial Average (Illustration 2-2) is presented here in the same manner as that used by the top Elliott Wave analysts.

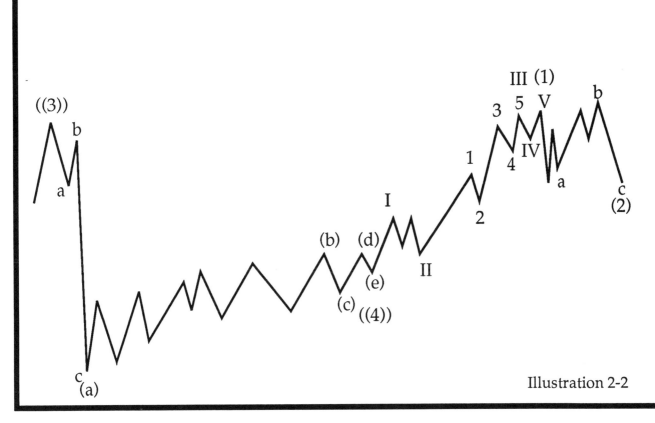

DJIA Weekly Chart. Elliott Wave Count. Version 1.

1. Notice the (a) (b) (c) (d) (e) set of counts, and explore the lack of balance.
   a. Between the counts (a) to (e) there are eight waves that are unaccounted for. This often has to be done to fit a market to the Elliott Wave Theory.
   b. Wave (e) is half the size of wave (c). If any wave can be ignored or matched randomly with another wave, there cannot be any foresight validity to the theory or method of analysis.
2. Retracement wave b at the end of the chart is higher than wave (1).
   a. Is the "b" wave an extension wave?
   b. Is it a retracement wave?
   c. How far should we anticipate wave (2) to go down?
      Because the Elliott Wave Theory lacks objectivity, it cannot answer these questions except with hindsight.

This second version of the Elliott Wave Count (Illustration 2-3) is substantially different, but also anticipates that this market will unfold differently. There are too many if's and maybe's. If this happens, then maybe that, or if that happens, then expect this. There is no concrete commitment. The market is either going up or down. A trading tool should anticipate not only the direction of the next move with better than 50% accuracy (after all, flipping a coin will give you 50% accuracy), but also it should anticipate an entry price with a favorable profit-to-risk ratio, preferably at least 2 to 1.

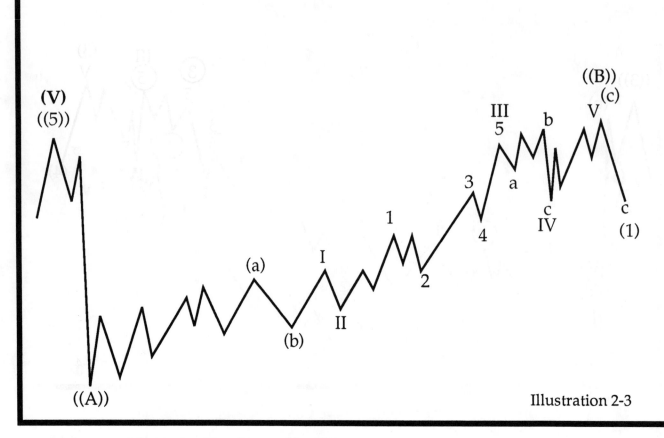

DJIA Weekly Chart. Elliott Wave Count. Version 2. 2/5/90

As mentioned earlier, the Elliott Wave Theory has alternative counts which add to the insecurity as to which stage of development a market is in. The chart in Illustration 2-2 is confusing; it leaves too much unknown. Add to this an alternative count, Illustration 2-3, which is completely different, and one's sense of security and confidence in the Elliott Wave Theory goes down.

Illustration 2-4 is a continuation of version one of the Elliott Wave Count from Illustration 2-2. As the DJIA weekly chart continues to unfold eight weeks later, the counting of Elliott Wave version one changes drastically.

The inconsistencies of this version of counting waves are as follows:

1. Waves II, 2, and 2 are similar in size, yet each one is assigned a different wave count.
    a. Wave 4 is half the size of wave 2.
    b. Wave IV is twice the size of wave II.
    c. Wave 4 is half the size of wave 2.
    d. Between wave (2) and wave (3), there were innumerable waves that could have been wave (3).

    Again, waves seem to be randomly matched in order to curve-fit a theory to markets.

2. With the exception of one wave, every wave count has changed, proving that as the market was unfolding previous counts did not hold up, and the current count does not have validity in real time trading.

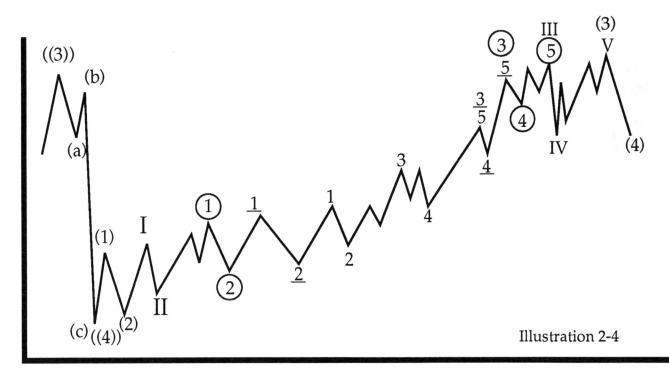

DJIA Weekly Chart. Elliott Wave Count. Version 1. 4/2/90

The next few charts that have Elliott Wave Counts are by a different Elliott Wave Theory expert. (The charts are from CQG. CQG provides data feed and various trading tools for clients' use. CQG in no way judges the merits of this or any analysis in this book.)

The next two Deutsche Mark weekly charts illustrate how the Elliott Wave count changed after only two months. Again, this indicates that the previous Elliott Wave count did not have much validity (see Illustration 2-5A and 2-5B).

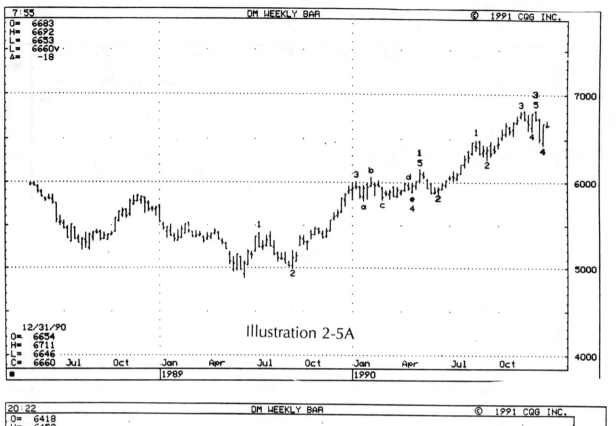

Illustration 2-5A

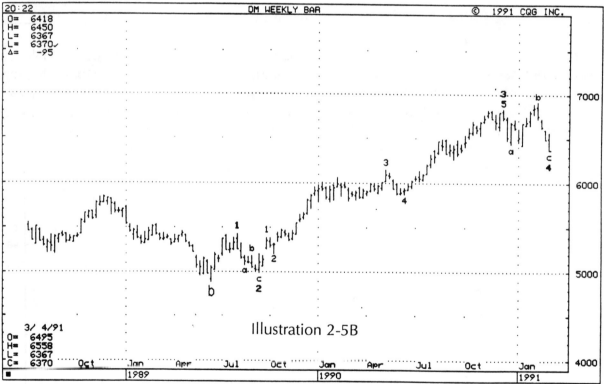

Illustration 2-5B

When the daily crude oil (Illustration 2-6) chart enters what Elliott practitioners consider either a major correction wave or a trend reversal, the Elliott Wave Theory is still looking for the "c" wave to balance the "a" and "b" waves that have been circled. While the Elliott Wave Theory is looking for the "c" wave, there have been potentially seven "c" waves which are numbered for identification. The complexity of numbering and lettering is confusing, imprecise, and has no clear objective organization. Does it really tell one what stage the market is in?

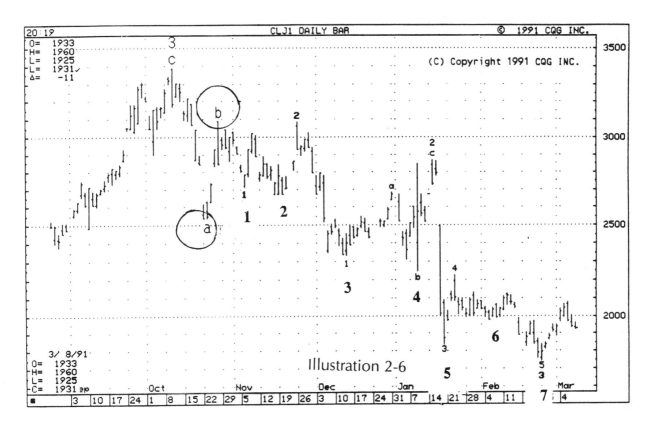

Illustration 2-6

Illustration 2-7 presents us with a daily Deutsche Mark chart. The wave that is labeled "b" in February is higher than wave 3. This way of counting waves is too confusing. At this point the Elliott Wave practitioner is waiting for wave 4 to be completed and then for an up wave 5. Wave 4 is greater in magnitude than wave "a" of December, yet wave 4 is supposed to be part of wave "a." This is too confusing and requires hindsight.

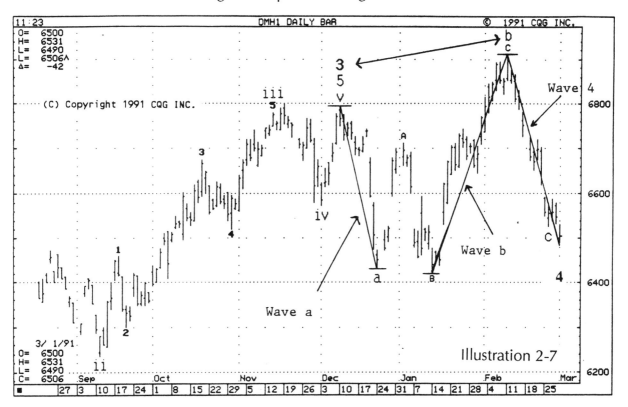

Illustration 2-7

The weekly Swiss Franc and weekly Dow Jones charts (Illustration 2-8A and 2-8B) illustrate how the Elliott Wave Theory, in order to fit a market to its theory, skips waves randomly. The waves that have been skipped are marked by <u>X</u>.

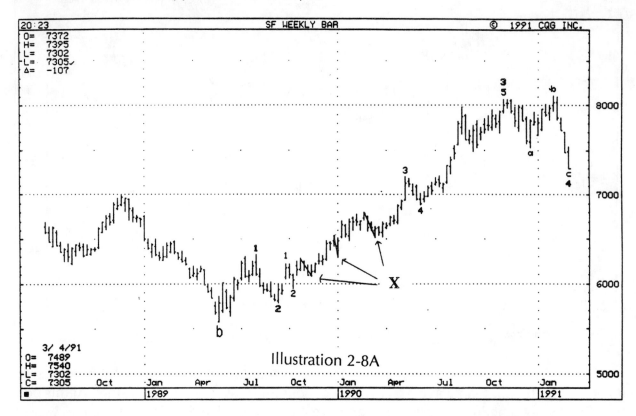

Illustration 2-8A

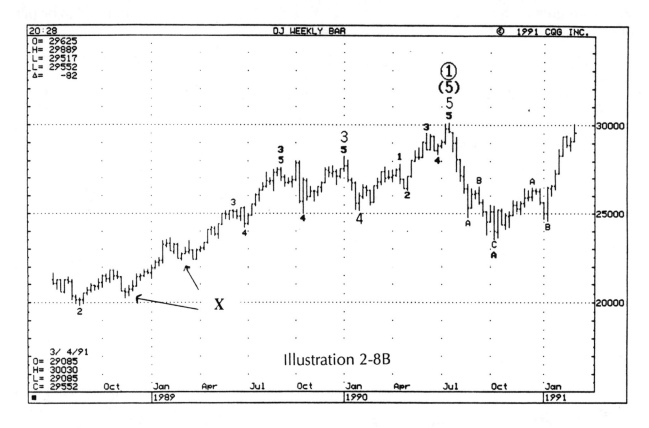

Illustration 2-8B

In the daily T-Bonds chart (Illustration 2-9), wave 4, circled to highlight it, is being matched by wave 2, also circled. When any wave can be matched by any other, there cannot be any objectivity or foresight. It all becomes guesswork. Wave 4 is twice the size of wave 2. If there is no rational order, how will one know which waves to match up, or how will one know the expected magnitude of a wave? Another example of this problem is demonstrated on the S&P 500 daily chart (Illustration 2-10). Wave 4, lined and marked, is twice the size of wave 2.

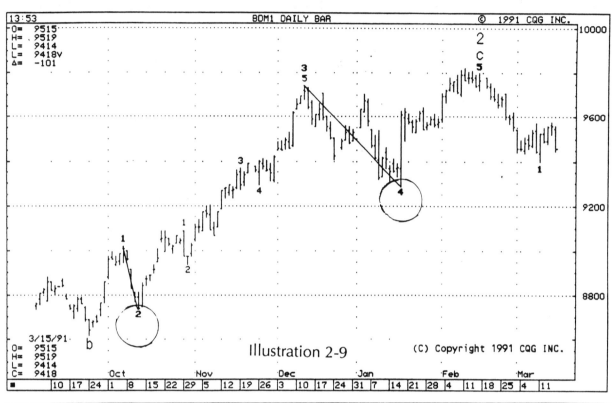

Illustration 2-9

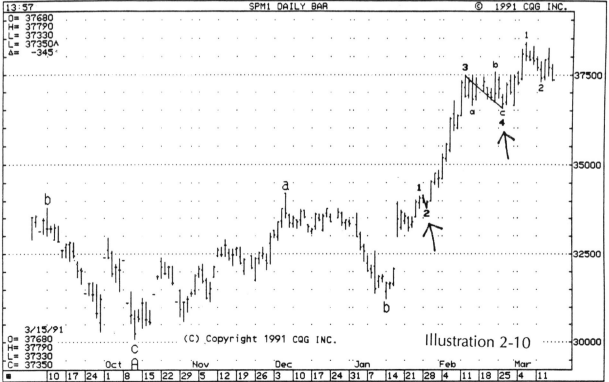

Illustration 2-10

19

I am grateful to Mr. Elliott for his theory. Perhaps without his observations, at the turn of the century, the Symmetry Wave Method may not have come into being, and it would not be possible to share this new method. I feel it was important to share examples of the Elliott Wave Theory so that it will be easier to understand the differences between the two theories. Another benefit you will gain from the comparison of the two theories is a conscious awareness of where the Elliott Wave Theory has its weaknesses and how the Symmetry Wave Method will overcome these shortcomings. The comparison of the two methods may also bring greater awareness of the difficulties which markets present to a trader.

Distinction Between The Symmetry Wave Method and Elliott Wave Theory

Symmetry Wave Method	**Elliott Wave Theory**
• Groups same magnitude waves together.	• Groups different size waves together.
• Builds perspective.	• Is an inadequate perspective builder.
• Symmetry provides for accurate anticipation of where a retracement will end.	• Does not provide for anticipation of retracement.
• Does not rearrange wave count except after a trend reversal (explained in Chapter Four).	• Rearranges wave count often.
• Usually has only one scenario for market development.	• Usually has several scenarios for market development.
• Has simpler rules for counting waves.	• Has complex and interchangeable rules for counting waves.
• Allows for objective trading. Rules are precise so all traders will count waves the same way.	• Is subjective, with variations in the wave count. Different traders interpret or label waves differently.
• Lets the market decide how many trend waves or retracement waves there will be.	• Tries to fit all waves into five trend waves and three retracement waves.
• For uptrend and downtrend, uses same method of counting waves.	• Uses complex numerical count for trend waves and complex alphabetical count for down-trend.
• Has specific rules for trend and trend reversal.	• Has no specific rules for trend or trend reversal.

Symmetry Wave Method (cont'd.)

- Organizes the markets, and is a specific trading tool.

- Accounts for all waves.

- Is simple and well defined, with less room for errors.

Elliott Wave Theory (cont'd.)

- Does not generate specific trades.

- Skips waves.

- Is too complex, leading to errors in judgment.

SECTION 2

SYMMETRY WAVE
The Method Itself

CHAPTER THREE

Rules For
The Symmetry Wave Method

Symmetry Wave may initially appear to be somewhat difficult, so it is important that you read the next three chapters carefully as they tend to clarify each other and make the overall concept quite understandable.

The Symmetry Wave Method is a system of rules for interpreting price fluctuations in stocks, stock averages, and futures markets, and it is a perspective builder. The method is both general and precise in its nature. In a general sense it helps us to understand overall market behavior. In its precision, the method not only predicts trend reversals, but often generates buy and sell signals with pinpoint accuracy.

Everything in nature has a repetitive pattern and a cycle. Without repetitive patterns, chemistry and physics would not be possible. Cycles abound in our lives, *i.e.,* night and day, heat and cold, birth and death.

In stock and futures markets, an up move in price is followed by a down move. This cycle is repeated in different magnitudes and manifests itself as waves on charts. The magnitude of these waves establishes patterns.

The Symmetry Wave Method singles out retracement waves of similar magnitude and groups them under the same hierarchy. The above rule is the essence of the Symmetry Wave Method. This one simple rule organizes the stock and futures markets, eliminates guessing wave counts, lets the market reveal its own intentions rather than fitting the markets to a theory, establishes a clear perspective, and reveals trend and trend reversals. It is a trading tool, and it follows the markets' own rhythms. This method lets a market unfold any way it wishes. A trend may develop in five, seven, nine, or eleven waves. It is irrelevant how many waves there are. Our concern is to match waves that have the same magnitude and to trade off of them.

NOTE: When following the examples given in this book, it will be important for you to refer to the illustrations often and properly follow the wave identifications. For example, we will be referring to wave 2 being matched by wave 4 and subsequently wave (2) being matched by wave (4). Therefore, to get the gist of what is being said, it is important to distinguish, for example, between wave 4 and wave (4). Also, most examples use uptrend, but all rules apply to downtrend as well.

Illustration 3-1 identifies each wave, and Illustration 3-2 shows proper labeling for this set of symmetrical waves during an uptrend. Illustration 3-3 depicts a downtrend with proper wave identification.

The American Heritage Dictionary defines symmetry as: "Beauty as a result of balance or harmonious arrangement." As the word "symmetry" implies, the Symmetry Wave Method is the grouping of waves that are similar in size, thus creating a balanced way of monitoring the unfolding of a market. Markets have a rhythm, and the Symmetry Wave Method defines the balanced rhythm and counting of that rhythm.

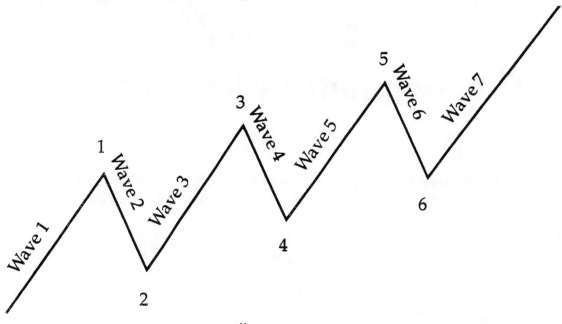

Illustration 3-1

Only one level of hierarchy

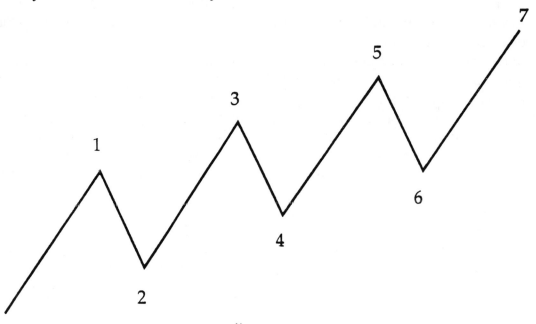

Illustration 3-2

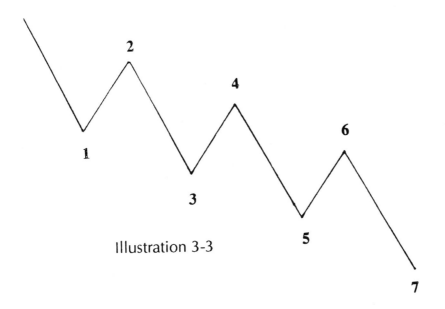

Illustration 3-3

THESE ARE THE RULES OF THE SYMMETRY WAVE METHOD:

Trend Wave and Retracement Wave

All price fluctuations fall into two categories: a price fluctuation, or wave with the trend, is called a **trend wave**; and a price fluctuation against the major trend is called a **retracement wave** (see Illustration 3-4 through 3-6). Trend waves are always labeled with odd numbers, and retracement waves are always numbered using even numbers. It is by contrasting the retracement waves to the trend waves that we start to organize the markets and to build a perspective.

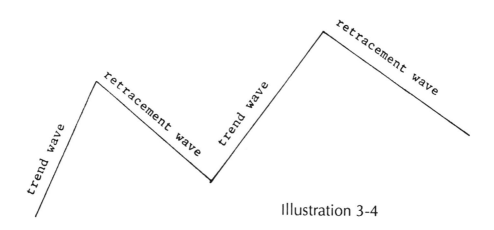

Illustration 3-4

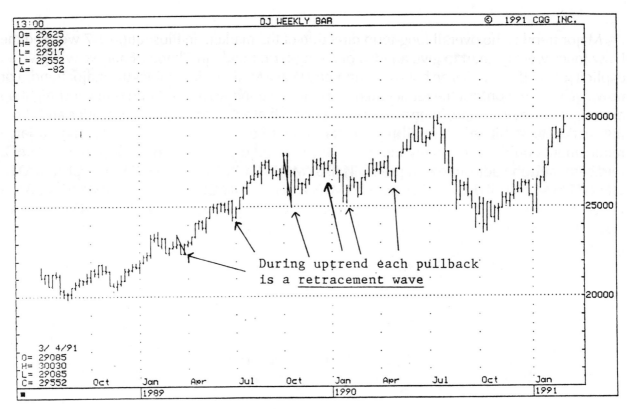

Illustration 3-5

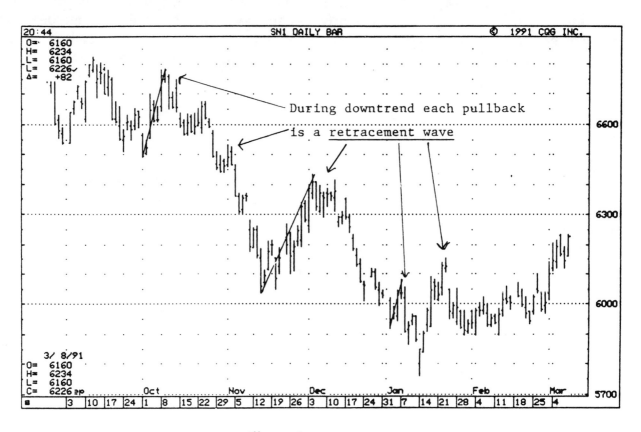

Illustration 3-6

Major trend is the overall long-term direction of the market. In Illustration 3-7 we used the Dow Jones weekly chart to give an idea of a long-term trend. In Chapter Four we will give an explicit rule and examples on how the Symmetry Wave Method determines the major trend. For now, we wish to contrast the retracement wave to the trend waves. A trend is never straight up or straight down. There are intervening retracements that adjust for any excess in price and allow the market to stabilize. A small retracement could be for only a few minutes, and a large retracement could last for many months. This is an adjustment in time. The magnitude of a retracement is the adjustment in price. **THE SYMMETRY WAVE METHOD CONCENTRATES ON THE MAGNITUDE OF PRICE ADJUSTMENT, THE RETRACEMENT. THE SIMPLICITY AND ELEGANCE OF THIS METHOD IS IN SINGLING OUT RETRACEMENT WAVES OF SIMILAR MAGNITUDE AND GROUPING THEM UNDER THE SAME HEADING.** The Symmetry Wave Method only attempts to group retracement waves; it is not important to group trend waves, nor does the method attempt to do so.

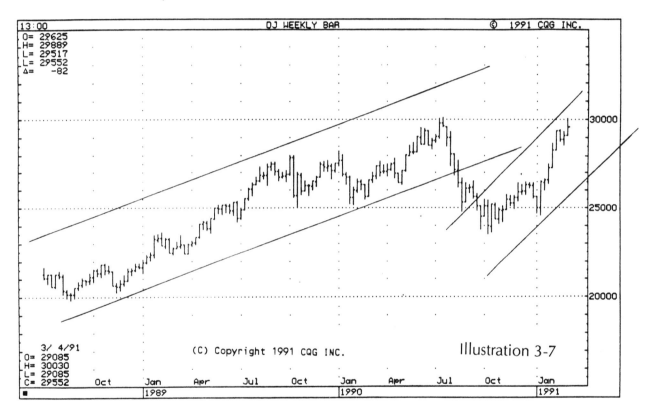

Illustration 3-7

Labeling of Waves

Among so many waves in a trend, the purpose of the Symmetry Wave Method is to lift out the same size *retracement* waves and group them together — to match apples to apples and oranges to oranges.

Four levels of hierarchy, or grouping of similar-sized waves, is usually the most a trend will develop. Therefore, four levels of hierarchy have been created. If a market develops in more than four sets of symmetrical waves, then more labels could be created as needed. All the labels for the different sets of symmetrical waves are numerical. The bigger waves are labeled with the higher hierarchical numbers, level one being the highest.

These are the labels to be used for grouping similar magnitudes of retracement waves:

27

Level One	(I), (II), (III), (IV), (V), (VI), (VII), (VIII), (IX), (X), (XI)
Level Two	I, II, III, IV, V, VI, VII, VIII, IX, X, XI
Level Three	(1), (2), (3), (4), (5), (6), (7), (8), (9), (10), (11)
Level Four	1, 2, 3, 4, 5, 6, 7, 8, 9, 10, 11

The grouping of waves and the heading under which a set of retracement waves are assigned is relative to the other sets of symmetrical waves. The set of symmetrical waves in Illustration 3-2 has been assigned 1, 2, 3, 4, 5, 6 and 7. They could have been assigned any of the other labels to indicate that these waves are similar in magnitude. The important point is the proper grouping of retracement waves and not the labels assigned to identify them.

As a market unfolds, waves will expand and subdivide causing reassignment of hiearchy, but the grouping of the waves will remain the same. Using the same charts in Illustrations 3-2 and 3-3, we will subdivide wave 3; this will compel us to assign the lowest hierarchy labels to the newly created set of symmetrical waves. The second level hierarchy label is assigned to the bigger set of symmetrical waves (see Illustrations 3-8 and 3-9).

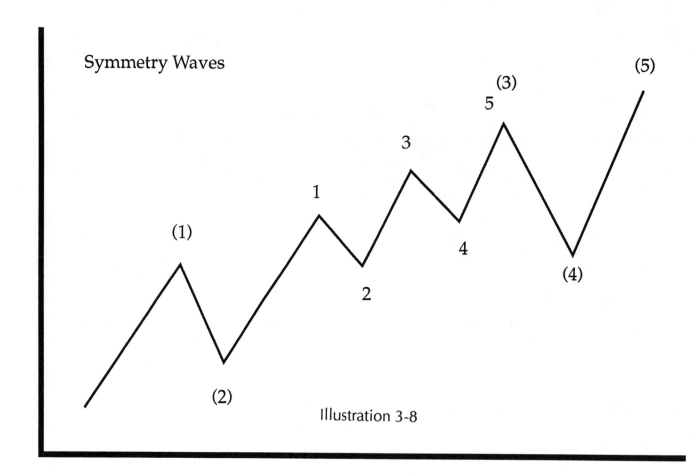

Symmetry Waves

Illustration 3-8

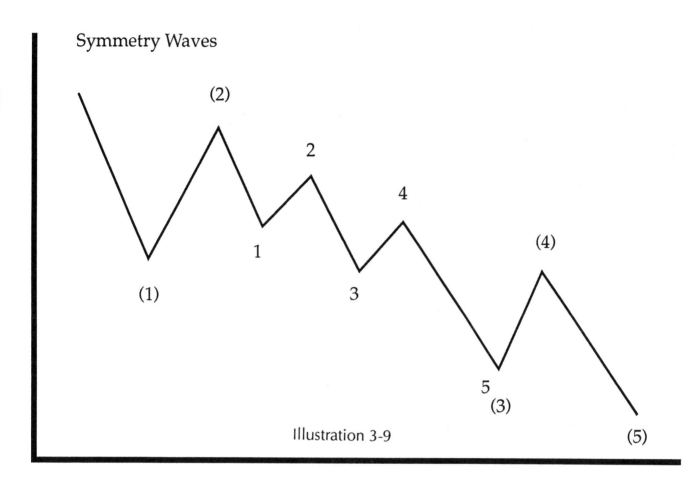

Symmetry Waves

(2)

2

4

(4)

1

(1)

3

5

(3)

Illustration 3-9

(5)

Waves of any degree in any series can be subdivided and re-subdivided into symmetrical waves of lesser degree. In Illustration 3-10A, an uptrend starts with a big retracement. In anticipation of smaller sets of symmetrical waves developing, we assigned to the first retracement hierarchy Level Three, which is I and II. Later the market develops a smaller retracement wave (2), which then is followed by even a smaller retracement wave 2. At this juncture three sets of different-sized symmetrical waves are developing. As the market unfolds, each set has a corresponding symmetrical wave (see Illustration 3-10B).

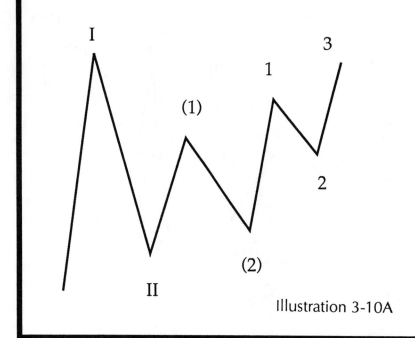

Illustration 3-10A

Symmetry wave pattern with smaller symmetry wave patterns in between.

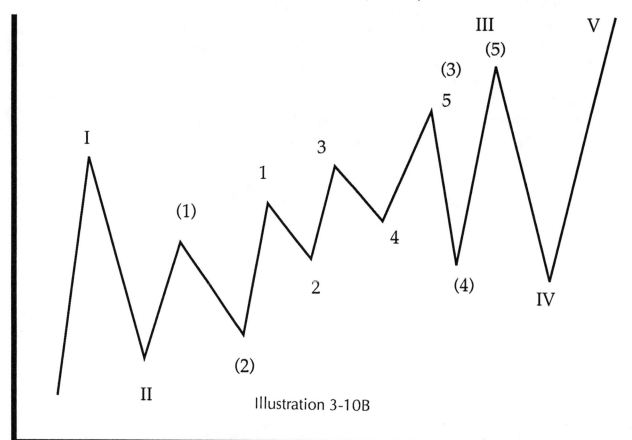

Illustration 3-10B

Just as markets can subdivide into smaller sets of symmetrical waves, conversely a market can expand into bigger sets of symmetrical waves. As the chart in Illustration 3-10B continued to develop and the previous three sets of symmetrical waves were completed, the market expanded into a bigger set of symmetrical waves (I), (II) and (III) (see Illustration 3-11).

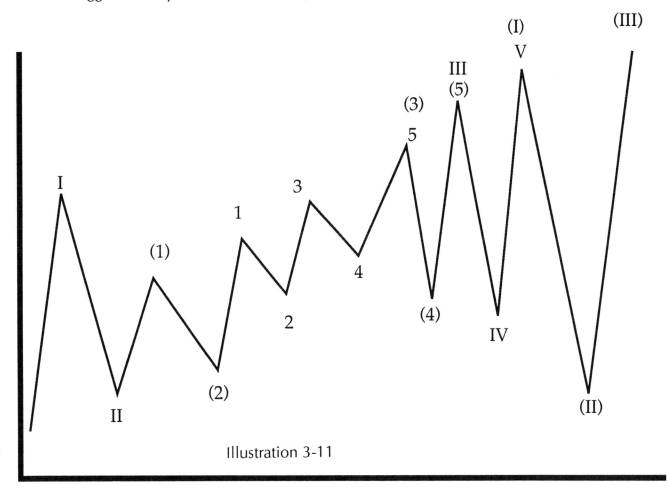

Illustration 3-11

In this section we are *not* trying to illustrate the proper labeling of the waves, but rather to establish the proper way to group waves. In the next few illustrations we will not label the waves using the Symmetry Wave Method. Note that waves that are grouped together do not have to be exactly the *same* size, but they need to be *similar* in size. The rule that applies here is that for two waves to be considered symmetrical, their magnitude must be within 20% of each other. The next two examples illustrate how this rule can be misused.

Assume the first retracement wave in Illustration 3-12A is 40 points. According to the 20% rule, if the next retracement is 32 points, we have symmetry between the first and second retracement. Now, look what happens to the third retracement if we make it 20% bigger than the first retracement (see Illustration 3-12B). This entire pattern, even though it is within the limits of the 20% rule, is not symmetrical; therefore, we need to establish more rules in order to make the Symmetry Wave Method more scientific. To make it fully scientific, however, would require too many rules. The key is building in enough structure to strike a balance between the art and the science. The art aspect will be conveyed to you by numerous examples over the next few chapters. However, on the next page are two more rules to help us group retracements more scientifically. Remember, the guiding scientific principle is to match the same magnitude of waves, while the art is to train your eyes to see the matching waves without calculating.

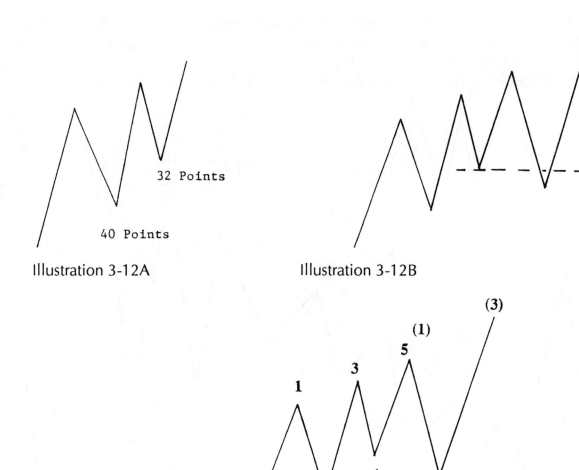

Illustration 3-12A
32 Points
40 Points

Illustration 3-12B

Illustration 3-13

First, a retracement wave cannot go below a previous retracement wave and both be part of the same group of retracement waves. Going back to Illustration 3-12B, the third retracement is below the second retracement; thus, these two retracements cannot be grouped together. Illustration 3-13 demonstrates the proper wave count. Second, the 20% rule is calculated from the original wave (wave number two) that the symmetry wave count starts from. Otherwise, there would be ever shrinking or expanding waves which would destroy symmetry. To further clarify the 20% rule, two more examples will be used. The second retracement is 20% smaller than the first retracement, and the third retracement is 20% smaller than the second retracement. This renders retracement three 35% smaller than retracement one and makes these waves asymmetrical (see Illustration 3-14).

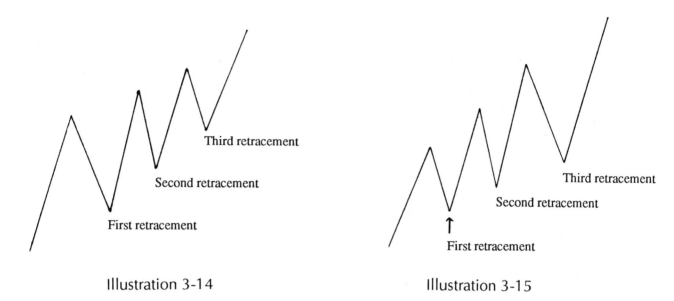

First retracement

Second retracement

Third retracement

Illustration 3-14

First retracement

Second retracement

Third retracement

Illustration 3-15

Conversely, the same problem would apply to expanding each subsequent wave's magnitude by 20%. The third retracement ends up being 44% greater than the first retracement (see Illustration 3-15). Again, the key is that a group of waves should be symmetrical to each other.

Illustration 3-16 uses a weekly Deutsche Mark chart to further illustrate the proper grouping of symmetry waves. All four levels of hierarchy are used in this chart. By using the Symmetry Wave Method, the possibility of confusing different magnitudes of waves, such as I, II, III, IV, and V waves with (1), (2), (3), (4), and (5) was eliminated. In mid-1989, waves I and II were developed. Following the rules of the Symmetry Wave Method, we can expect a wave IV that would match wave II in magnitude. This knowledge helps us keep the proper wave count and keeps us with the major up-trend. Between waves II and IV, there were several sets of smaller symmetrical waves.

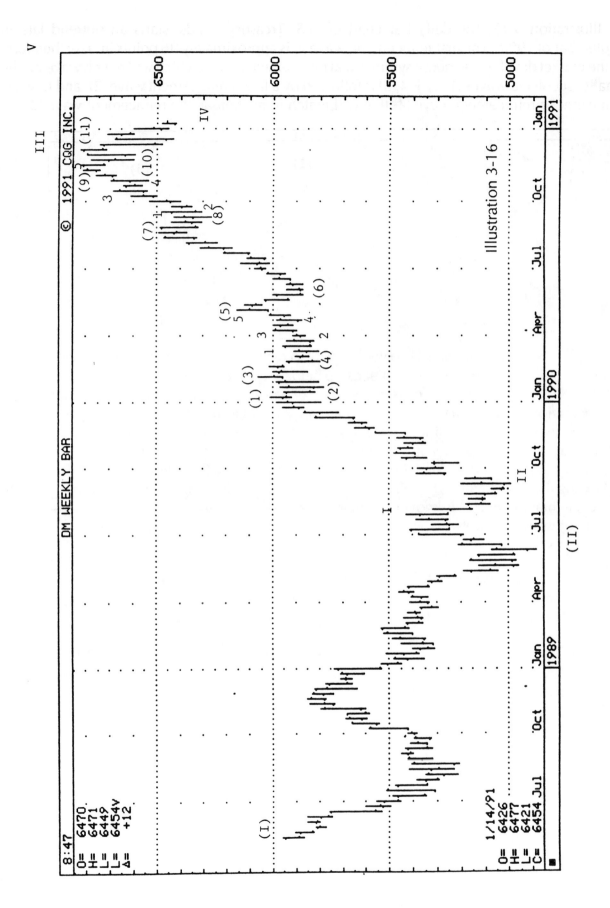

Illustration 3-16

Illustration 3-17, the daily bar chart of U.S. Treasury Bonds, starts an uptrend late in September of 1990. The first retracement, wave 2, is approximately 96 points in size; therefore, as the market develops, expect a symmetrical retracement wave 4 which will match wave 2. The smaller set of five waves (1, 2, 3, 4, 5) is followed by a larger retracement wave (2), and now we can expect a retracement wave (4) that will match in magnitude the retracement wave (2).

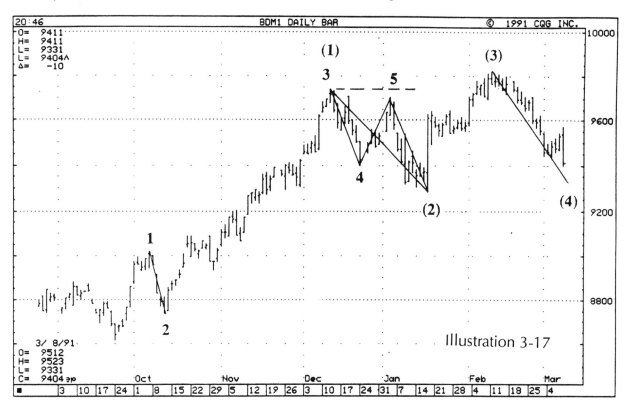

Illustration 3-17

Failure Wave

In the above illustration, the smaller set of wave counts ended with a failure wave.

Failure wave, also known as failure swing, is the term used when a wave fails to exceed a previous wave (wave 5 failed to exceed wave 3) (see Illustrations 3-18 and 3-19). A failure wave is a common occurrence and often brings about confusion rather than a solution. Some people feel that a failure wave during an uptrend is a sign of weakness and, conversely, a sign of strength during a downtrend. Research has shown failure swings to be about 50% accurate in predicting a trend reversal.

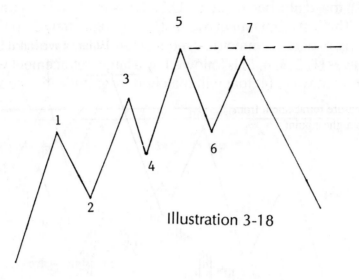

Illustration 3-18

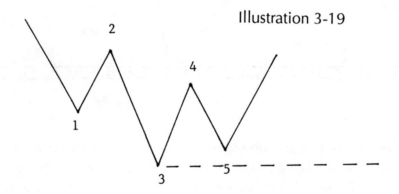

Illustration 3-19

During failure waves it is important to look at the entire size of a wave and not to measure the magnitude of a retracement from where the failure wave ended (see Illustrations 3-20 and 3-21).

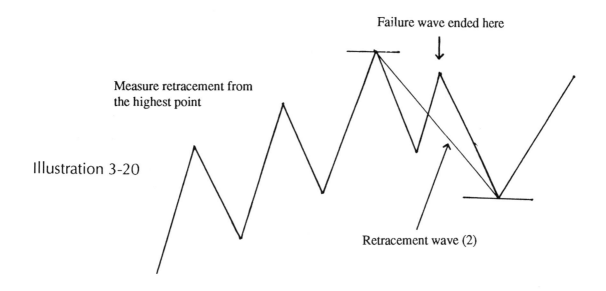

Failure wave ended here

Measure retracement from
the highest point

Illustration 3-20

Retracement wave (2)

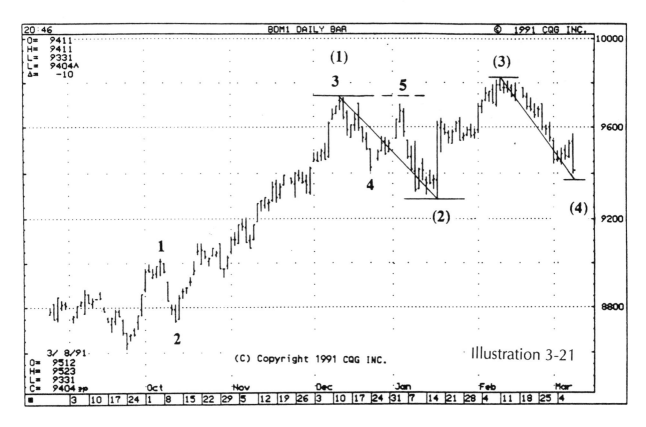

Illustration 3-21

No Matching Symmetry Wave

A smaller set of symmetrical waves is always found inside a bigger set of waves, as seen in previous illustrations. Illustration 3-22 depicts the wrong way of trying to group retracement waves. The two smaller retracements before and after the bigger retracement wave 4 *cannot* be grouped together. That is to say, there cannot be intervening bigger waves between a set of smaller waves.

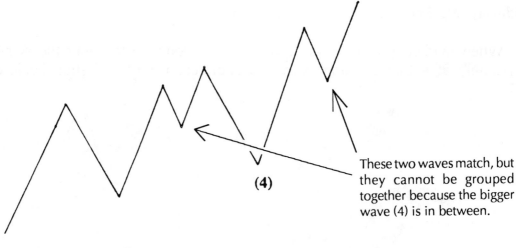

These two waves match, but they cannot be grouped together because the bigger wave (4) is in between.

(4)

Illustration 3-22

At times, during a trend, for a particular retracement wave there will be no matching symmetry wave. In these situations, do not try to force the wave count. Rather, start a new set of symmetry wave counts. With the Symmetry Wave Method we let the market decide what it is doing. The process of following the unfolding of markets should be as natural as possible and as least contrived by human imagination as possible.

If a wave does not have a corresponding symmetrical wave to create a symmetry and it is followed by a retracement wave that fits into the next hierarchy of symmetry, then a new wave count starts. For example, in Illustration 3-23, the first retracement does not have a corresponding symmetrical wave. Since the second retracement wave is in a different hierarchy, we start a new wave count and wait for a symmetry. And in Illustration 3-24, the second retracement does not have a corresponding symmetrical retracement wave, and it is followed by a third retracement that matches the first retracement. Therefore, the first and third retracements are grouped together, and the second retracement does not have a corresponding symmetrical retracement wave.

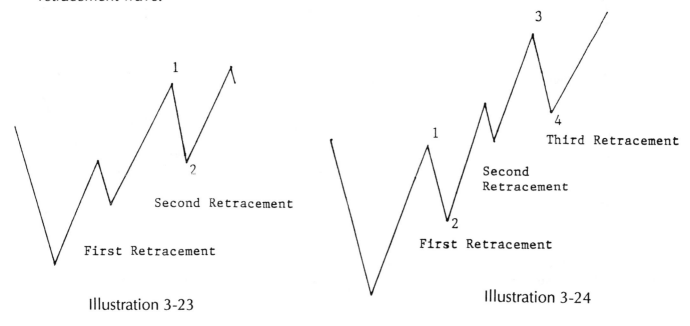

Illustration 3-23

Illustration 3-24

Sideways Market

When markets go sideways or consolidate, continue to count the symmetrical waves separately rather than as a single wave. The correct counting is illustrated below (Illustration 3-25).

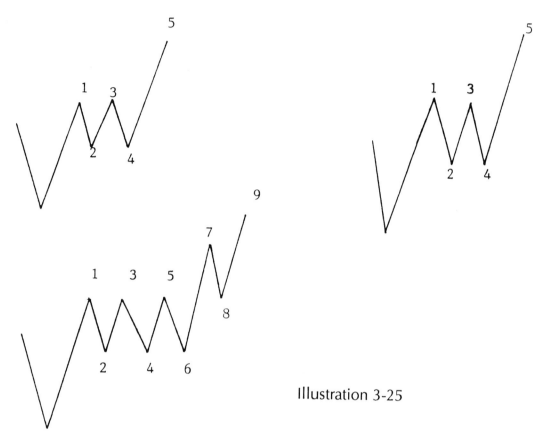

Illustration 3-25

A unique part of the Symmetry Wave Method is that during an uptrend as well as a downtrend, the same system of wave counting is used. This makes for an easier and more accurate organization of price fluctuations.

CHAPTER FOUR

Trend and Trend Reversal

Even though the Symmetry Wave Method has precise rules, it is subject to subjective interpretation. Analyzing charts with this method depends on practice and on experience. In this chapter we will show numerous examples of the Symmetry Wave Method in use.

As with any method of trading or analysis, the Symmetry Wave Method has its limitations. One of these limitations is that since a market can develop in five, seven, nine or even eleven symmetrical waves, it is not possible to know in advance at which wave count the market will end its trend.

It is best to focus on trading with the trend for two reasons. First, if you are anticipating a trend reversal or analyzing when to trade against the major trend, then you are not analyzing with the major trend. Remember from Chapter One, the mind can only see one perspective at a time. The mind is either interpreting waves to rationalize to go against a trend, or the mind is analyzing the waves to go with the trend. It cannot do both at the same time. If it analyzes in both directions, then this leads to compromise and compromise leads to confusion. Second, there is only one day that a market makes the top, but there are many days to the top, so statistically it is best to trade with a major trend. By trading with the major trend, the question of how many waves a trend will have becomes relatively irrelevant. At all opportunities, trade with the major trend.

Since we do not know when a trend will top or bottom, we wait for the trend to confirm its reversal.

HERE IS THE RULE TO DETERMINE THE TREND:

If the current retracement is bigger in magnitude than the previous largest big retracement, and if the market closes beyond the previous big retracement wave, then the trend has reversed.

In Illustration 4-2, the trend has developed in seven waves. Subsequently the market goes beyond retracement wave 6 to reverse its trend. The dash line indicates the price at which the trend reverses from up to downtrend. Illustration 4-2 demonstrates the trend reversing from down to up.

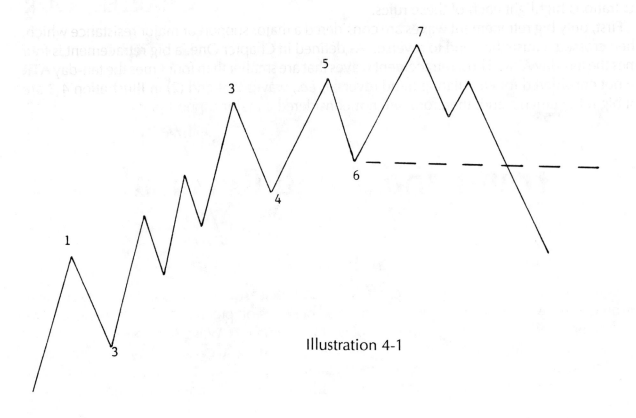

Illustration 4-1

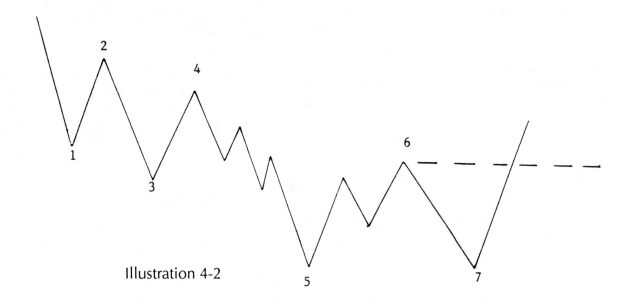

Illustration 4-2

The rule to determine the trend actually has three rules within it, and the next several illustrations highlight each of these rules.

First, only big retracement waves are considered a major support or major resistance which, when crossed, cause the trend to reverse. As defined in Chapter One, a big retracement is four times the ten-day ATR. Thus, retracement waves that are smaller than four times the ten-day ATR are not considered for calculating trend reversal, i.e., waves 2, 4 and (2) in Illustration 4-3 are not big retracements and, therefore, are not considered a major support price.

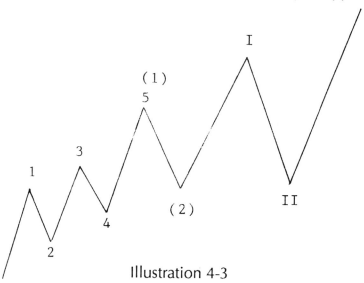

Illustration 4-3

Second, the current retracement wave should exceed in size the previous retracement wave. For example, if a trend had three major retracements that were 80, 90 and 85 points, then the current retracement has to be more than 90 points for a trend reversal to be in effect. In Illustration 4-4, waves (2) and (4) are larger than waves 2 and 4; thus, the current retracement must exceed in magnitude waves (2) and (4) to fulfill this rule of trend reversal.

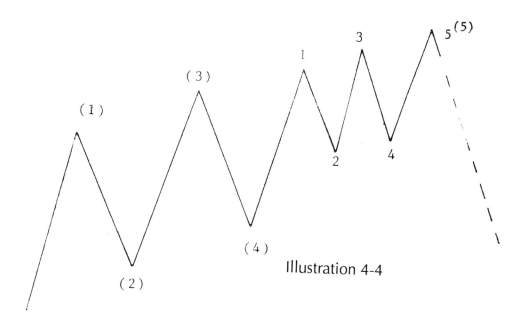

Illustration 4-4

The third rule is that the market needs to close beyond the previous big retracement wave. Illustration 4-5 uses a daily Deutsche Mark chart as an example. The retracement wave IV which lasted from November of 1990 to January of 1991 is the latest major support price, and on March 8, 1991, the market closes below the retracement wave IV, thus effectively reversing the uptrend to a downtrend.

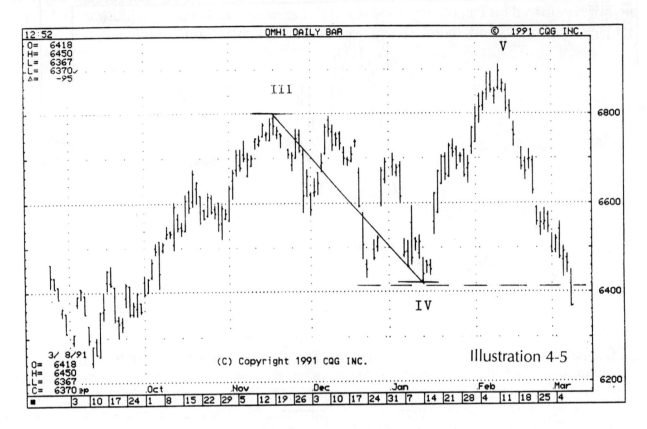

Illustration 4-5

Because all wave counts start at the beginning of a new trend, it is of the utmost importance to get a good grasp of when and where a new major trend begins in order to properly count symmetry waves. We will use several markets to illustrate trend reversal and the subsequent proper counting of waves (and changing of labels).

Illustration 4-6 uses a daily crude oil chart. On October 23, 1990, this market ends a big retracement which is bigger than previous retracements (see Illustration 4-7). Subsequently, the market rallies for six weeks and fails to make new highs, and after several weeks closes below the big retracement of October 23, 1990. Thus, the trend has effectively reversed to the down side. Illustration 4-8 shows the proper new wave count with the downtrend. Wave I and II are followed by wave III, which has subdivided into a (1), (2), (3), (4), (5) wave count. The subsequent short rally (wave IV) balances wave II. Downtrend wave V so far has two sets of symmetrical waves in it.

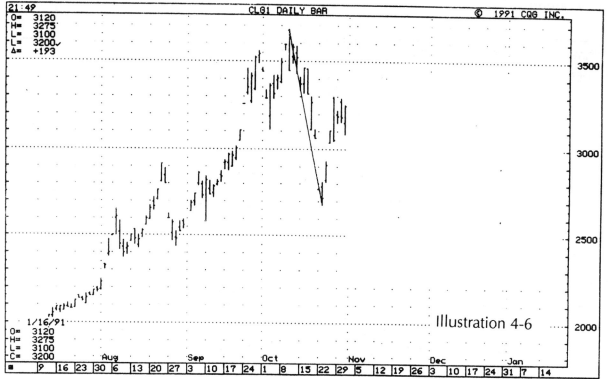

Illustration 4-6

Illustration 4-7

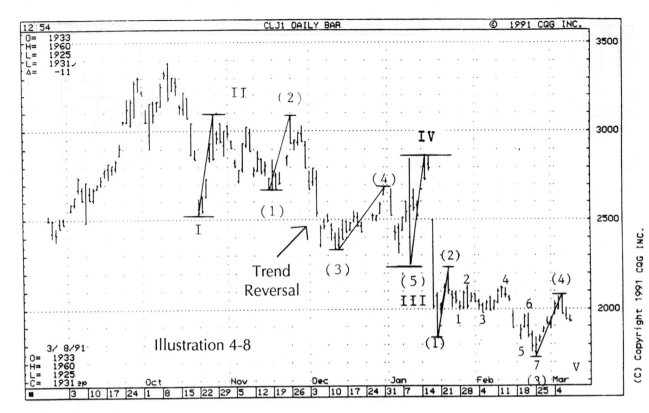

Illustration 4-8

The weekly Swiss Franc chart in Illustration 4-9 continues to illustrate trend reversal. In May of 1989, the Swiss Franc bottoms and starts its uptrend until February of 1991. During this period the biggest retracements are wave II and wave IV. Thus, we need a retracement bigger than wave II and IV. The price at which the trend will reverse is the bottom of wave IV. A few weeks later the Swiss Franc starts to tumble and closes below symmetry wave IV. The trend has reversed to the down side (see Illustration 4-10).

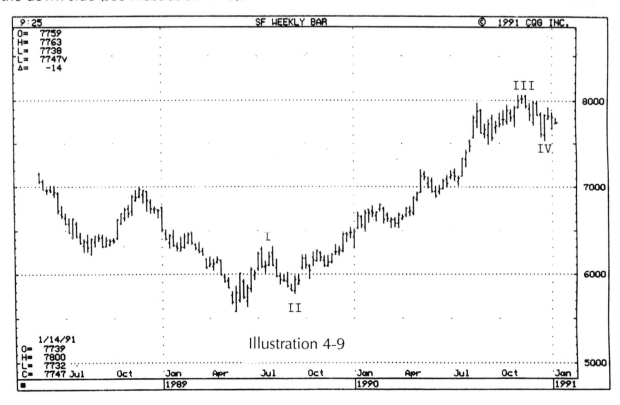

Illustration 4-9

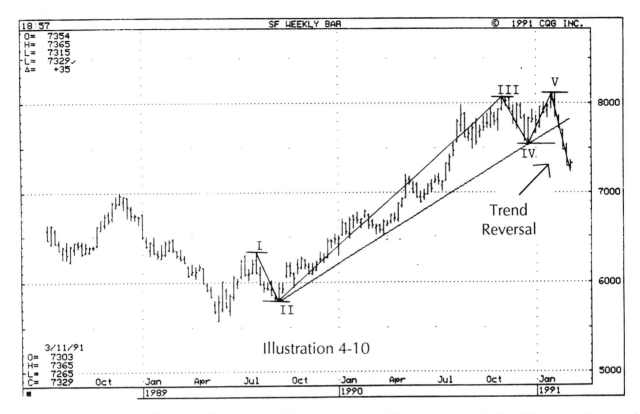

Illustration 4-10

In the next example, we will use a weekly sugar chart (Illustration 4-11A) to illustrate the trend reversal and the subsequent symmetry wave counts. Up until the end of April 1990, the trend is up, and the Symmetry Wave Method is currently counting trend wave IX. Notice how each previous retracement wave is symmetrical in size, therefore making it easy to identify the proper grouping and labeling.

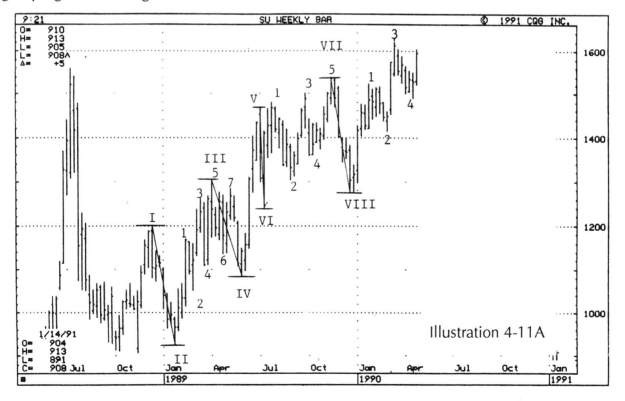

Illustration 4-11A

47

This market is extremely overdeveloped, and since there rarely are nine or eleven waves, especially of the magnitude of these retracement waves, we can expect a trend reversal. During the eighteen-month uptrend, the largest retracement was 2.74¢. This figure is subtracted from the top, which is at 16.27¢ (see Illustration 4-11B). Since it closed below the big retracement wave 4, the trend reversal is confirmed. Subsequently, the downtrend on the weekly sugar chart has developed into five big downtrend waves containing several smaller sets of symmetry waves.

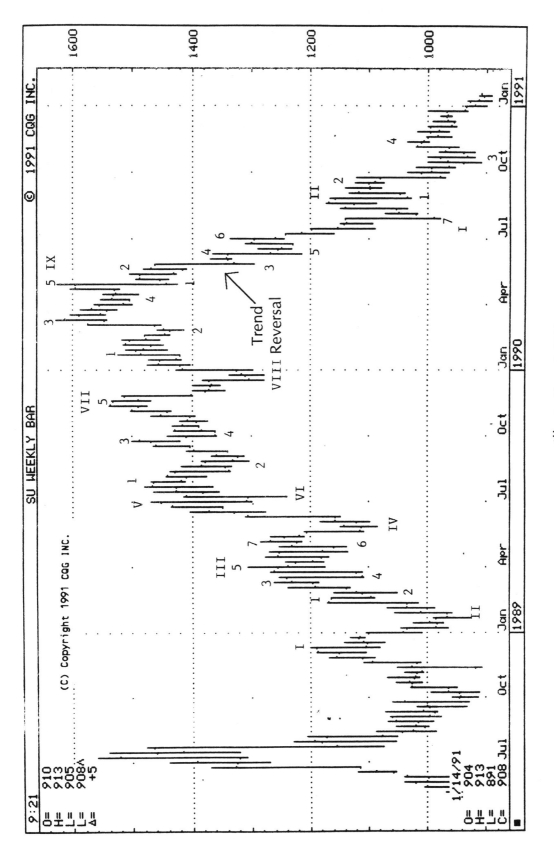

Illustration 4-11B

The daily chart of copper in Illustration 4-12A indicates a potential trend reversal because the retracement wave number (VI) exceeds the smaller retracement wave number 4. However, looking at the weekly copper chart (see Illustration 4-12B), we see that retracement wave number (VI) matches the previous big retracement waves (II) and (IV). At this juncture, is the trend up or down? Your decision will depend on your trading style and how aggressive you wish to be. Personally, the observation that I abide by is that the trend does not reverse easily; thus, it is best to wait for confirmation of trend reversal and to follow the trend reversal rule given earlier. Because the retracement wave VI did not exceed in magnitude the previous big retracement wave II and IV, the trend is still down. Currently, the copper market is developing downtrend wave IX. This market is overdeveloped, and we can either expect a trend reversal or a retracement bigger than wave VI.

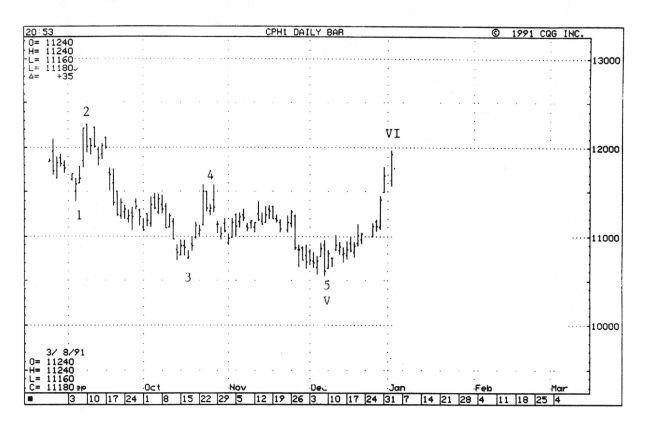

Illustration 4-12A

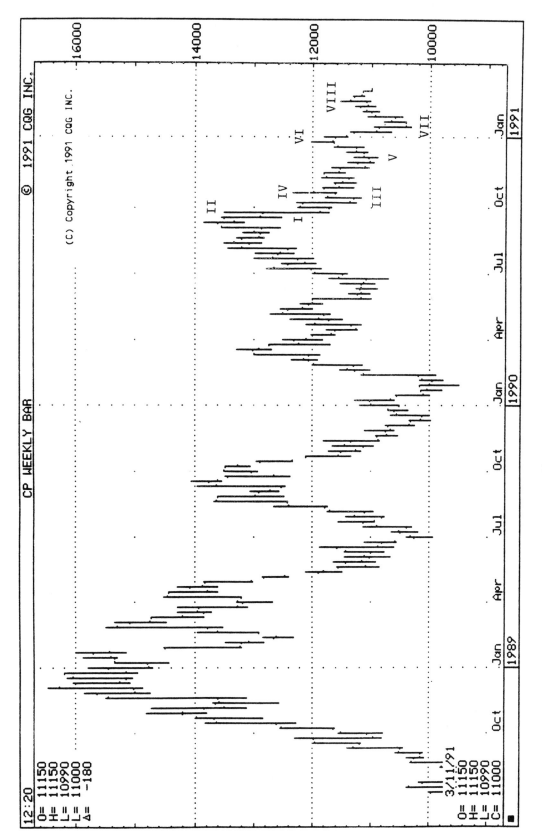

Illustration 4-12B

CHAPTER FIVE

Trading Using The
Symmetry Wave Method

Trend lines, channel lines, Gann lines, moving averages, moving average crossovers, the stochastic indicator, the relative strength indicator, MACD, Fibonacci ratios and breakouts are all terms you are probably somewhat familiar with, since they comprise most of the more popular methods and indicators. Why is it that these tools never seem to work consistently (even in combination)? Basically it's because they do not have the intelligence to discriminate between trending and sideways markets, they don't make the necessary adjustments for differing wave magnitudes, and they can't isolate trend reversals accurately. An indicator's function is to move up and down based on price action relative to the past few (or many) days. This up-and-down action goes on regardless of whether the market is in a sideways or trending mode, thereby generating random unintelligent trading signals. The end result is an excess number of losing trades and no real perspective on how a market is behaving.

The efficiency of trading, namely, accuracy and profit-to-loss ratio, increases by knowledge-ably entering a market after determining the trend, and waiting for the market to either finish its sideways price action or retracement. This is a markedly different approach from relying on one indicator (or a combination of them) under all conditions.

All entries into a market fall into two categories:

1. Later entry: Entering a market as it is moving in the direction one wants.
2. Early entry: Entering a market as it is retracing; in other words, anticipating a bottom or top.

In conjunction with the Symmetry Wave Method, both categories of entry will be explored. However, before we jump into analyzing entry methods, the subject of trading with the trend versus against it will be looked at one more time.

This book is geared towards helping a person trade with the trend; therefore you'll find almost all of our examples are entries with the major trend. It is my observation that trend waves are larger than retracement waves. Also a trend wave is usually longer in duration than a retracement wave. Therefore, statistically, it is best to focus one's attention on a trade with the trend.

In the previous chapter we discussed the shortcomings of not knowing where a trend will end. We resolved this issue by waiting for the trend to reverse itself by closing below the previous major support price. The second major unknown is that since markets do expand into bigger symmetrical waves and subdivide into smaller symmetrical waves, it is not possible to know for sure the magnitude of the current retracement. However, the very premise of the Symmetry Wave Method resolves the question about the magnitude of a retracement wave. If you remember, the entire idea is to wait for the current retracement to match, in magnitude, a previous retracement. As an example, if the previous retracement was 100 points, then we wait for a subsequent retracement that is approximately 100 points (see Illustration 5-1). However, if there is an intervening retracement, let's say 60 points, then we would first expect a subsequent retracement that would match 60 points (see Illustration 5-2), followed by a 100-point retracement to match wave (2).

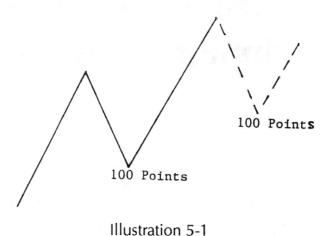

100 Points

100 Points

Illustration 5-1

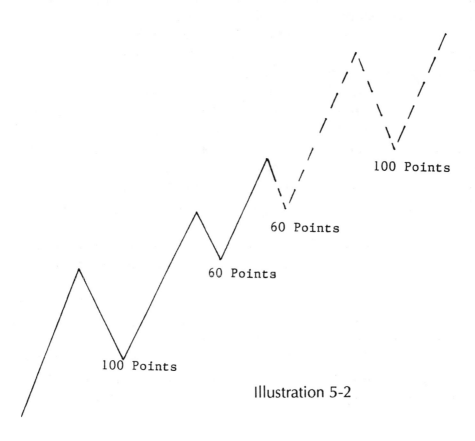

100 Points

60 Points

60 Points

100 Points

Illustration 5-2

Markets often behave with such precision. When they do not, a losing trade may be generated. Research has shown that if you trade with the major trend and wait for a matching symmetry wave, the accuracy of the trades is greater than 50%, with a favorable profit-to-loss ratio of more than two to one.

Going back to our examples, after the first 100-point retracement, there are at least three possibilities. First, you may choose to trade the intervening 60-point retracement second, you could opt to trade only the 100-point retracement. The third possibility is that the market may retrace more than 100 points or reverse its trend (see Illustration 5-3).

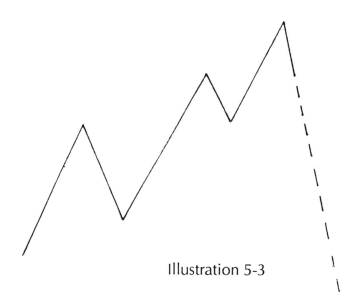

Illustration 5-3

However, experience (and commonsense) indicates that the simpler the trading program, the easier it is to trade, with the least number of mistakes creeping in. Even though the Symmetry Wave Method is a complete trading system in and of itself, other trading tools can be used with it.

Now let's turn to entry methods, starting with the early entry method since this will be the basis for late entry methods.

Early Entry Method

Early entry requires the trader to anticipate a bottom and to put a buy order in before the market reaches the target. If one waits to see what the market will do after reaching an anticipated target, then it is no longer early entry, it is a late entry. Symmetry is established when a market reaches 80% of the magnitude of a previous wave. However, entering the market at the 80% mark is too early. The 20% rule is an efficient way to group similar-sized waves, but not efficient enough for early entry. With the early method it is suggested that you wait for the current retracement to match at least 90% of the previous symmetric retracement before entering the market. However, do not enter earlier than 3/4 of a 10-day ATR. The idea is to enter a market before it reaches the symmetry price, but not to enter too early.

By following the aforementioned guidelines the profit potential is increased, while the size of the necessary protective stop is reduced. In Illustration 5-4, the 80%, the 90%, a hypothetical protective stop and a hypothetical profit target are marked. As you can see, entering at the 90% mark requires a smaller risk, yet makes a bigger profit.

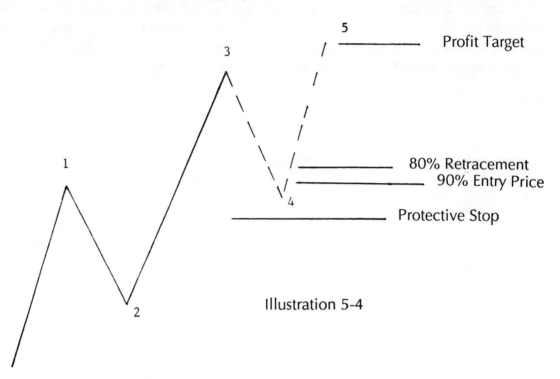

Illustration 5-4

In Illustration 5-5A, the Standard & Poor 500 market is in an uptrend. Since wave 2 was established, this market has gone up for two months without a corresponding retracement wave 4. Retracement wave 2 is approximately 28.5 points. Thus, we need a retracement that is at least 25.6 points (90% of 28.5 points) to enter in anticipation of a bottom. In Illustration 5-5B, on April 17, the June S&P contract tops at about 393.50. From this figure we subtract 25.6 (90% of retracement wave 2). Thus, we are targeting to go long an S&P 500 contract at 367.90. On May 15 our target of 367.90 is reached and we would enter a long position.

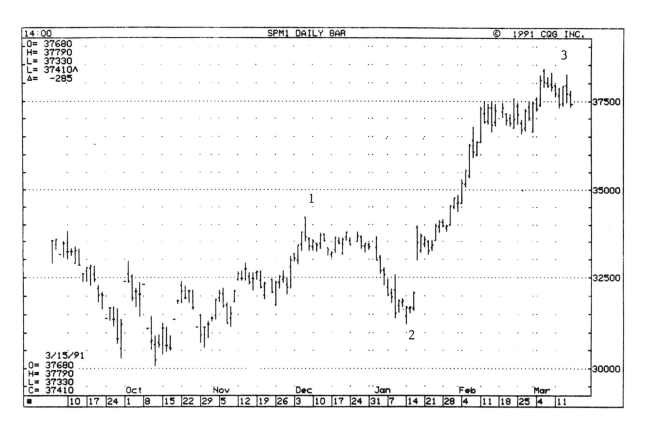

Illustration 5-5A

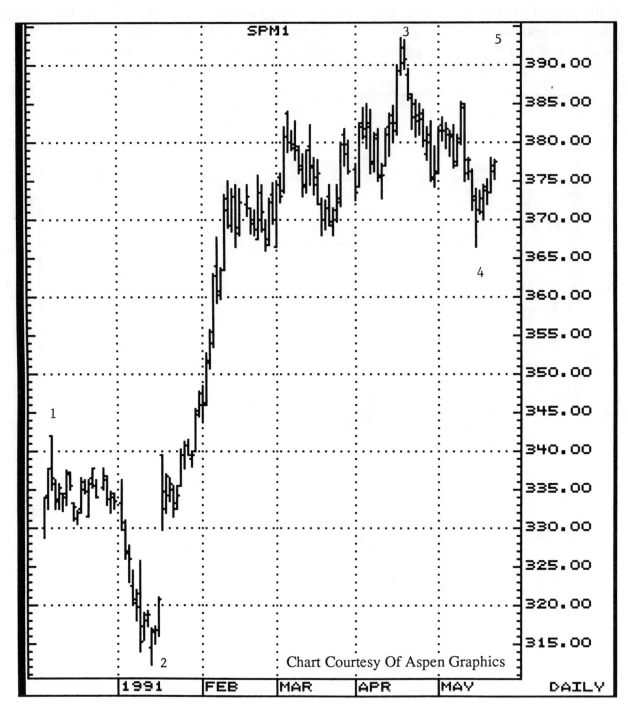

Illustration 5-5B

The daily Swiss Franc chart (Illustration 5-6) has reversed its trend in February to the downside, and in early April rallied approximately 330 points to create retracement wave 2. After wave 3 we would anticipate a rally of at least 300 points to enter short (approximately 90% of the previous symmetry wave). On April 29, wave 3 bottoms at .6666. To this price we add 300 points and come up with .6966 as our sell target to go short. On May 14, the 300-point rally target is reached and a short position is established. Subsequently, the market falls down to accomplish wave number 5.

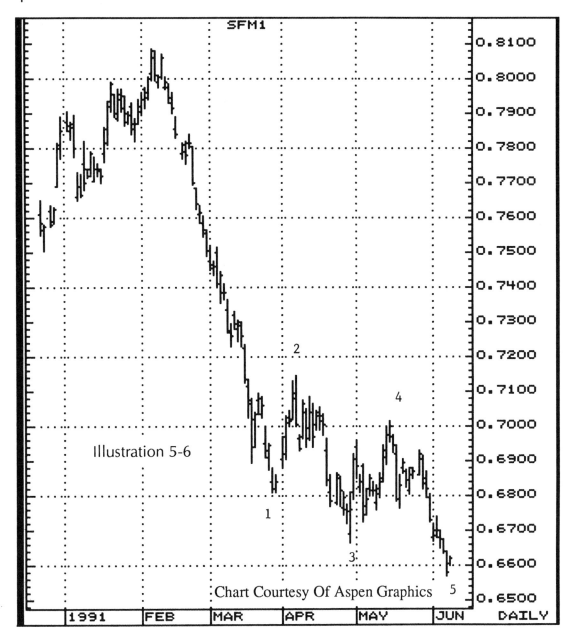

To further illustrate aggressive trading, we will use a weekly Gold chart and trade off a gigantic symmetry wave (see Illustration 5-7). The magnitude of wave II is approximately $67. After trend wave III we expect the retracement wave II to be balanced by a similar size wave. For early entry we would expect a retracement of at least 90% of $67, or $61. Wave IV is approximately $69 in magnitude — an excellent long-term short position with big profit potential and a relatively small risk.

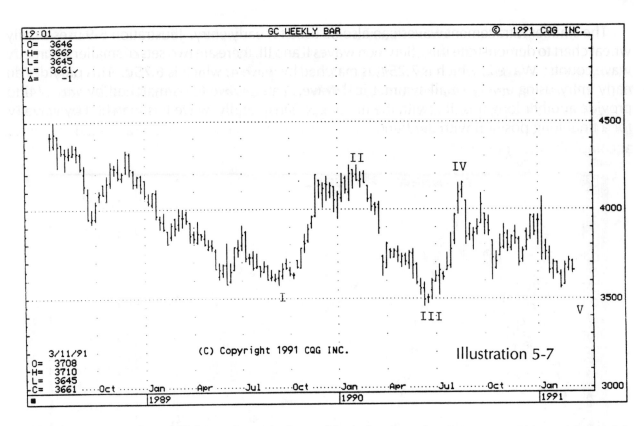

Illustration 5-7

At times some incredible trades can be achieved using the Symmetry Wave Method in conjunction with the early entry method, while taking only a relatively small risk. Illustration 5-8 presents a monthly Gold chart. In March of 1983, there is a retracement wave (IV). The trend wave (V) ends in February of 1985, and subsequently we have a retracement lasting 34 months that matches in magnitude the retracement wave (IV). The ensuing downtrend wave (VII) is approximately $150 in magnitude.

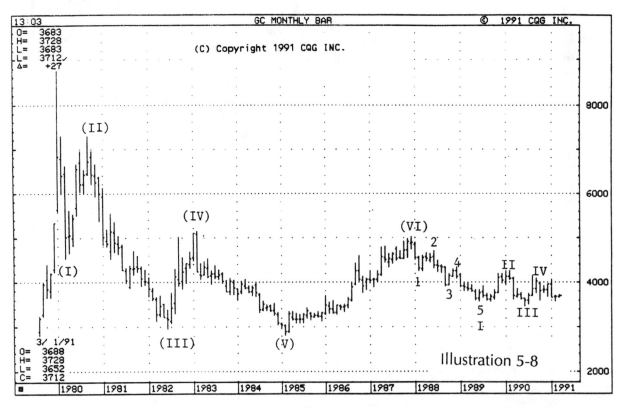

Illustration 5-8

The smaller retracement waves can also be used for early entry. Illustration 5-9 uses a daily wheat chart to demonstrate this. Between waves II and III, there are two sets of smaller symmetry wave counts: Wave 2, which is 7.25¢, is matched by wave 4, which is 6.75¢. This provides an early entry using a very small symmetrical wave. Later, wave (2) is matched by wave (4) to provide another long position with the major uptrend. Finally, wave II is matched by wave IV for a final long position with the trend.

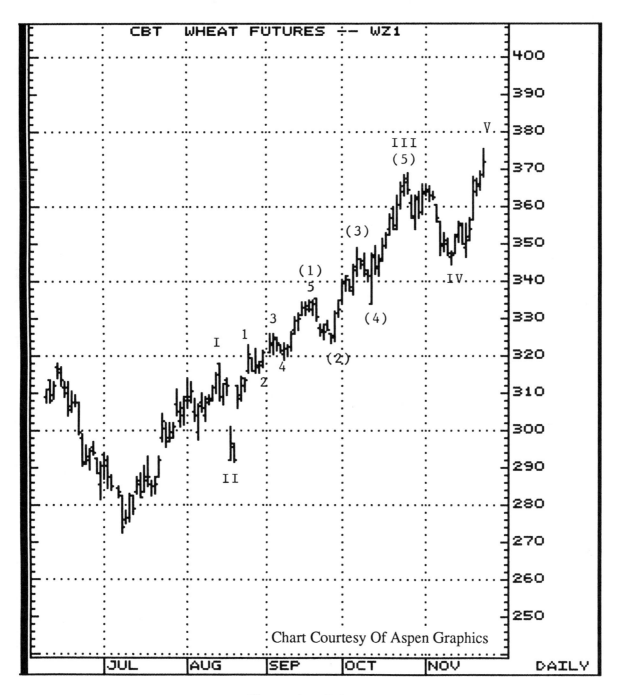

Illustration 5-9

Illustration 5-10, the daily Eurodollar chart, provides one more example of the early entry method. The major trend is up. In early June the market has a big retracement, followed by a rally and a mini retracement wave 2 on June 25. A four-day rally is followed by a symmetrical retracement wave 4, to provide a small risk investment with the uptrend. Wave 2 is 15 points in magnitude, and wave 4 is 16 points.

Illustration 5-10

The Symmetry Wave Method can be used to trade off gigantic waves, as in the monthly Gold chart, or off miniwaves, as in the Eurodollar chart. All sizes of waves are equally viable for establishing a position. Experience shows that it is best to put an entry order in before the market reaches the entry price. A common mistake among traders is the tendency to wait and see what the market will do. By then, the market has already done it, and it's too late. You have to put your orders in before the fact.

Late Entry Method

The decision on whether to use the early entry method or the late entry method should not depend on which method will produce better results, but on one's own nature. For some people, entering a market long when it is falling, without a bottom in sight, is too fearful, yet to others it is exciting and a challenge. To be successful in trading, it is important to use a style of trading that is suitable to your nature. Among other things, this may mean using a method that produces less profit but is within your comfort zone. Early entry and late entry have the same risk, but early entry produces greater profit since it takes advantage of the entirety of a trend wave.

When using a late entry method, like with the early entry method, you first must wait for a symmetry wave to be established. However, with the late entry method, a position is entered only when the market starts to move with the trend again. Once the symmetry is established, you must wait for the market to resume the move with the major trend. There are many degrees of waiting for a trend to be re-established. You could enter the market as soon as it starts to move with the major trend (Illustration 5-11), or you could wait for the market to substantially move with the major trend and only then enter the market (Illustration 5-12). To accomplish late entry, methods that were mentioned at the beginning of this chapter, among others, can be used.

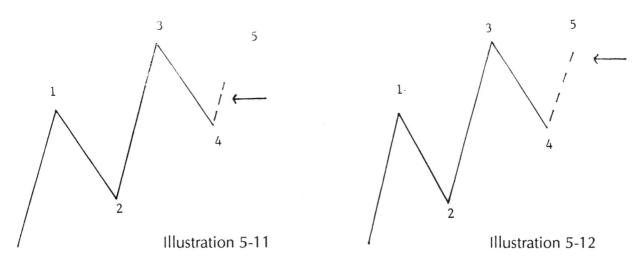

Illustration 5-11   Illustration 5-12

The same charts will be used for illustrating late entry as were used for early entry. For example, using the S&P 500 chart (Illustration 5-13), you could wait for wave 4 to match wave 2 and then use a nine-day stochastic crossover as an entry method. In this case, your entry would have been at the close of May 20, marked with an arrow. Another method may have been to use a three-day breakout. This would mean taking the highest high of the past three days and putting a buy order one or two ticks above the previous three days (see Illustration 5-14).

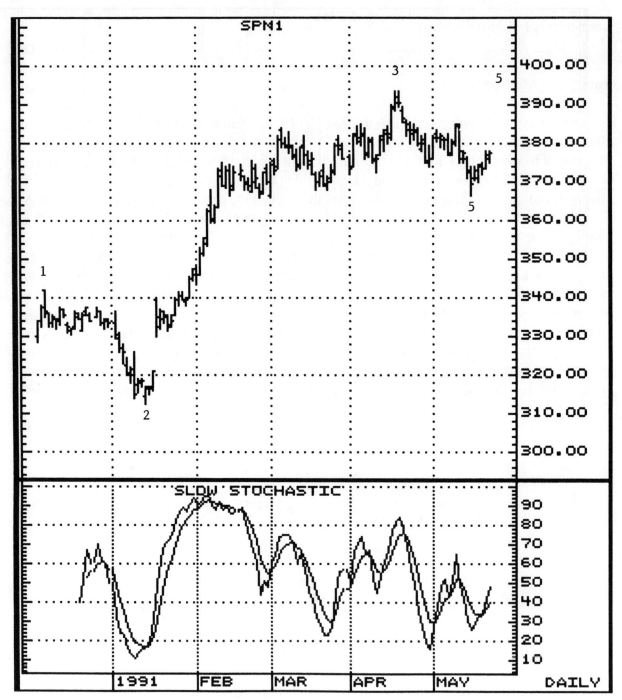

Illustration 5-13

Chart Courtesy Of Aspen Graphics

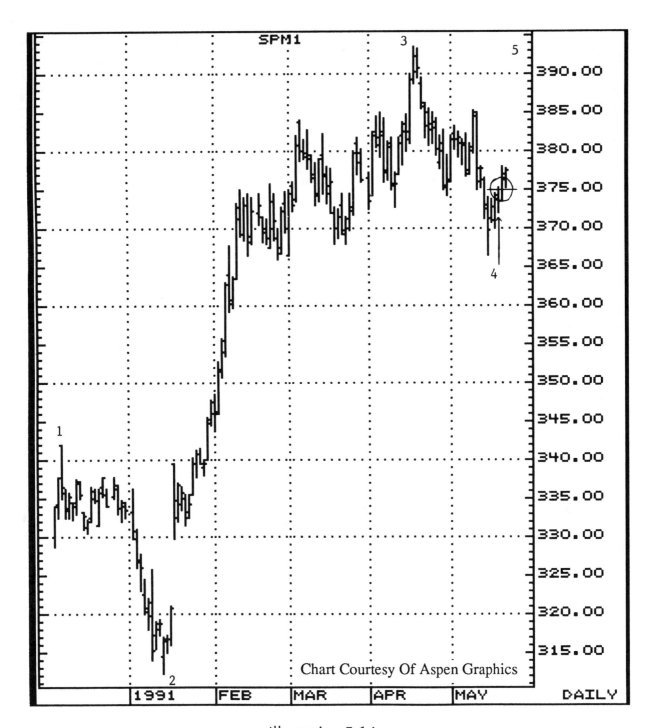

Illustration 5-14

Using the daily Swiss Franc chart (Illustration 5-15) after symmetry wave 4 was established, you could use a 10-day breakout, which is even more delayed than the stochastic crossover or three-day breakout. The benefit of an even later entry is that after a big retracement, the market has re-established its trend more firmly.

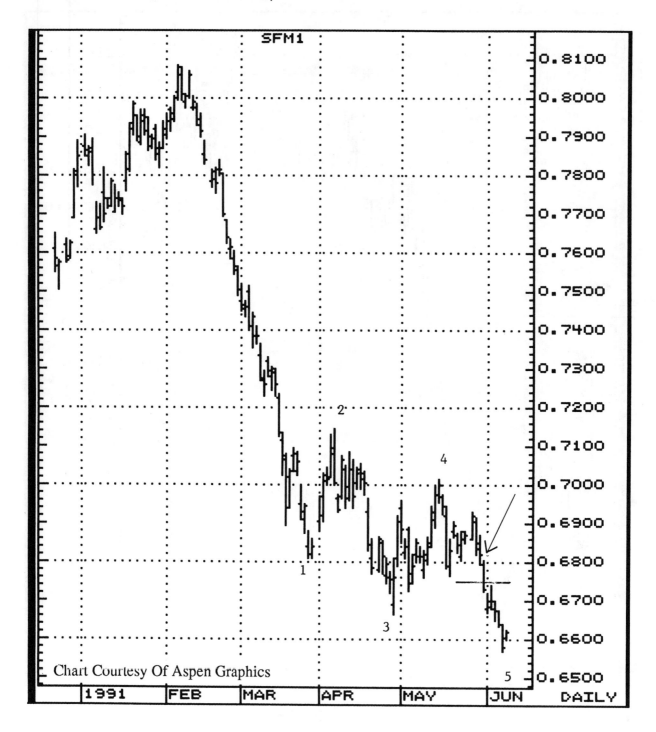

On weekly charts, one of my favorite late entry methods is to wait for the symmetry wave to establish itself and then to use a one-week breakout (see Illustration 5-16). Another method is to use a trend line, as in Illustration 5-17.

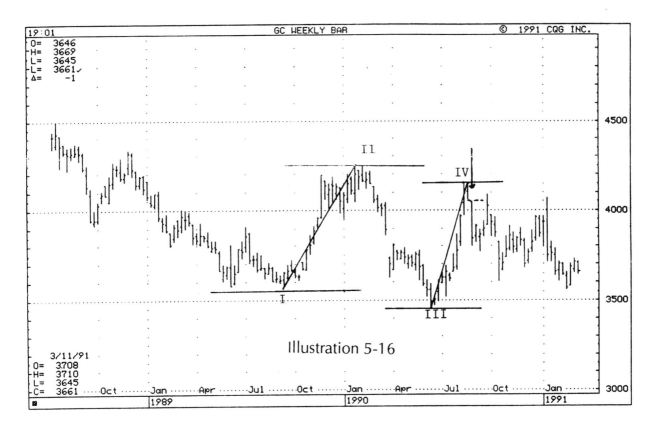

Illustration 5-16

Illustration 5-17

On smaller retracement waves, because the magnitude of the retracement is small, it is best to use a one- or two-day breakout as an entry method (see Illustration 5-18).

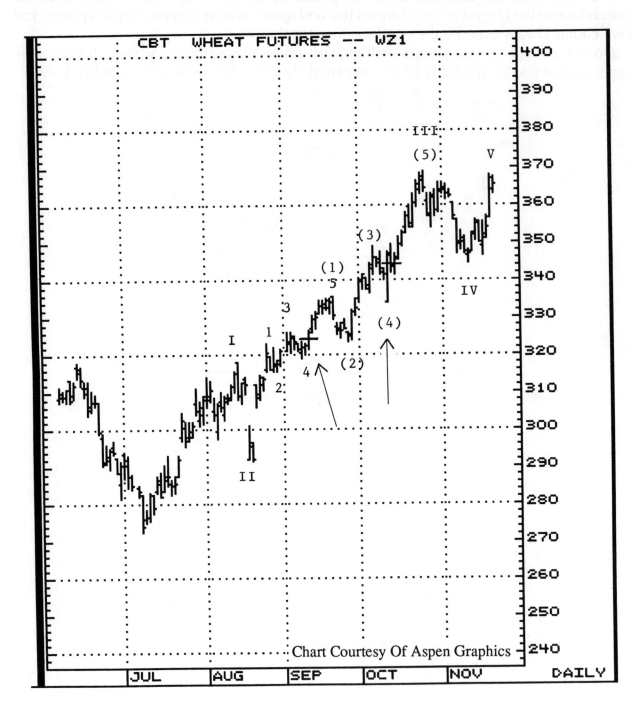

Illustration 5-18

Establishing a winning position takes a lot of effort. This is where mental fortitude and training come into play. It may take two or three tries before a big winning position is established. This requires patience and consistency. The most successful money managers keep doing what they know will work, even if it hasn't produced any profit for as long as eighteen months. This is how important it is for a person to be consistent. After two or three failed attempts, one big profitable trade will make up for the few small losers.

If at any time the counting becomes confusing using the Symmetry Wave Method, concentrate on the biggest group of waves first and ignore smaller groups. Bigger symmetrical wave counts always override the smaller symmetrical wave counts.

Do not attempt to base your overall analysis on smaller symmetry waves. It is strongly suggested that you keep weekly charts. Where daily charts fail, weekly charts will clarify.

CHAPTER SIX

Subdividing Retracement Waves And Labeling Them

In the previous chapters we have concentrated on the trend and the intervening retracement waves. You may have noticed that a retracement wave has many waves within it. These waves are called subwaves. Subwaves are always a part of, and within, the even-numbered retracement waves, and are identified using the alphabet (see Illustration 6-1). As with retracement waves, the bigger waves are labeled with the higher hierarchical letters, Level One being the highest.

Level One: (A), (B), (C), (D), (E), (F), (G).

Level Two: A, B, C, D, E, F, G.

Level Three: a, b, c, d, e, f, g.

Note: Because there are more waves with the trend, it is necessary to have four levels of hierarchy. Retracement subwaves are fewer, requiring only three levels of hierarchy.

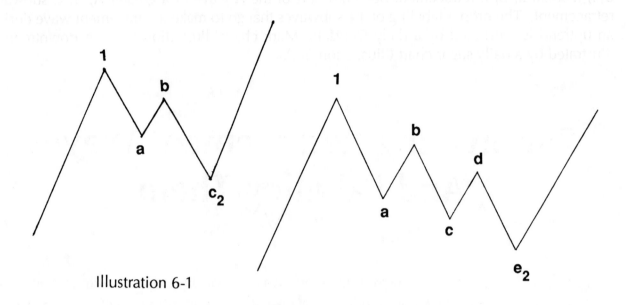

Illustration 6-1

A retracement wave can be made up of three, five, or more subwaves. In Illustration 6-2, retracement wave 2 is made up of three subwaves (a, b, c), and the symmetrical retracement wave 4 has five subwaves (a, b, c, d, e). Note that even though retracement wave 4 has five subwaves, it is symmetrical in size with retracement wave 2.

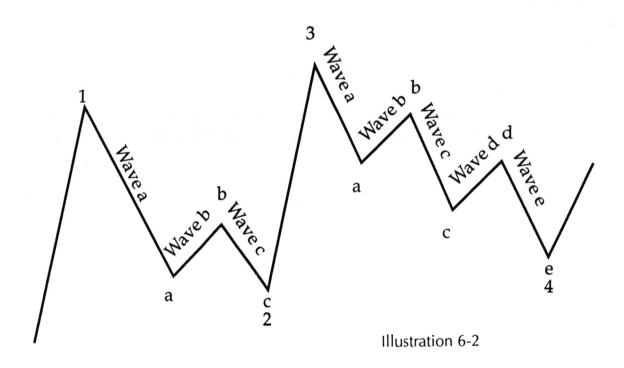

Illustration 6-2

A subwave can subdivide into smaller waves or become part of a subsequent bigger subwave. In Illustration 6-3, the subwave C has subdivided into five waves (a, b, c, d, e), and in Illustration 6-4, a small a, b, c retracement becomes part of the A wave of a greater A, B, C subwave retracement. The proper labeling of the subwaves that go to make a retracement wave during an uptrend is illustrated by a daily Deutsche Mark chart (Illustration 6-5). A downtrend is illustrated by a daily sugar chart (Illustration 6-6).

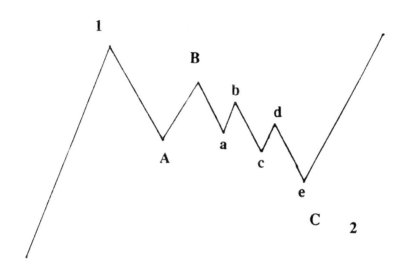

Illustration 6-3

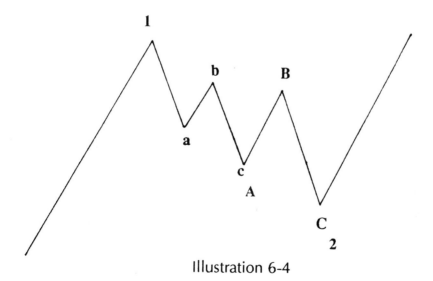

Illustration 6-4

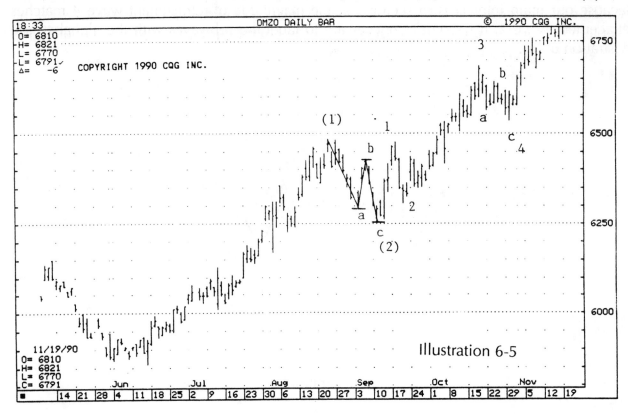

Illustration 6-5

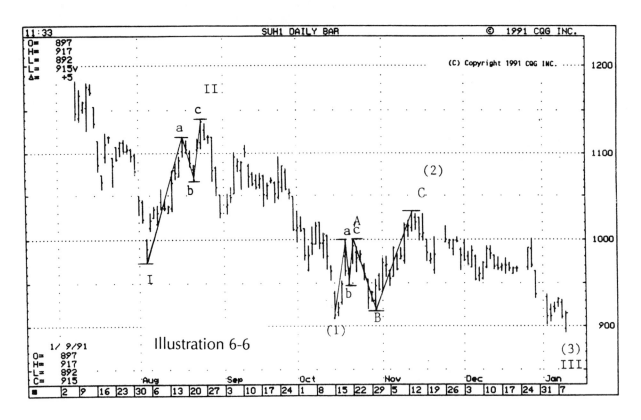

Illustration 6-6

Subdividing a retracement wave and labeling it with the alphabet is an important trading tool, but for proper counting of symmetry retracement waves it is not necessary. For example, Illustration 6-7A shows the proper numeric labeling and the alphabetical labels for the subwaves. Because our main interest is in seeing that the magnitude of retracement wave 4 matches retracement wave 2, it becomes unnecessary to label the subwaves with the alphabet (see Illustration 6-7B).

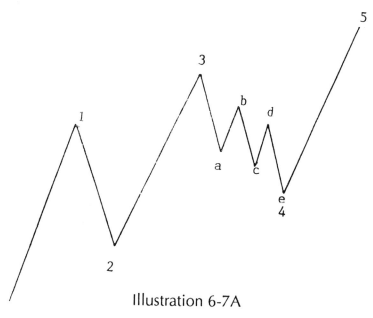

Illustration 6-7A

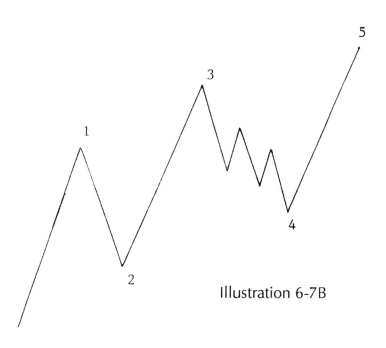

Illustration 6-7B

It is sufficient to wait for wave 4 to be similar in size to wave 2. Not having to label the subwaves that are part of a retracement wave simplifies wave counting and trading even more. However, since every trader will be using the Symmetry Wave Method differently, it is important to further illustrate proper labeling of subwaves. The illustrations that follow here show proper sub-labeling of retracement waves.

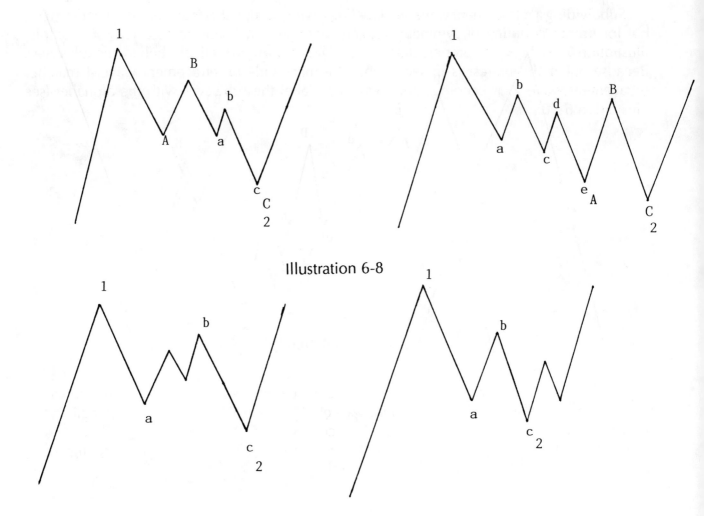

Illustration 6-8

Illustration 6-9 demonstrates an extremely complex retracement wave 2 that is made up of three levels of hierarchy of subwaves. Occurrence of three levels of subwaves is rare.

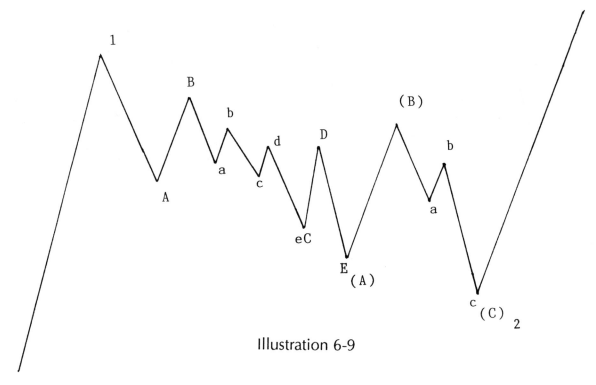

Illustration 6-9

Just as trend waves can have a failure wave, so can subwaves. These failure subwaves (Illustrations 6-10A and 6-10B) occur approximately 25% of the time and indicate strength in the direction of the major trend. A failure subwave occurs when "c," "e," or "g" wave fails to exceed a previous subwave within the same retracement wave. The dashed lines highlight the occurrence of a failure wave.

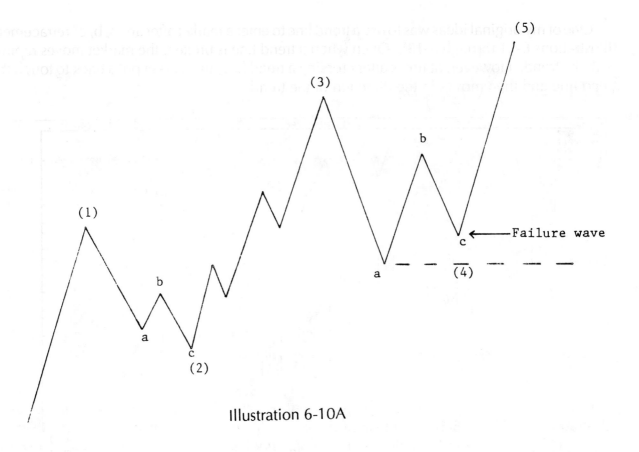

(5)

(3)

(1)

b

c ← Failure wave

a

(4)

a

b

c

(2)

Illustration 6-10A

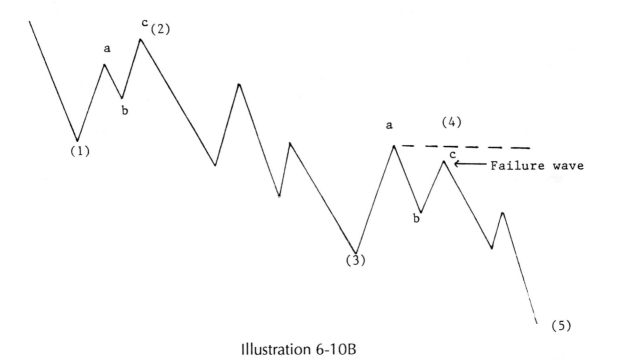

c (2)

a

b

(1)

a

(4)

c ← Failure wave

b

(3)

(5)

Illustration 6-10B

One of my original ideas was to use a trend line to enter a market after an "a, b, c" retracement (Illustrations 6-11 through 6-13). Often when a trend line is broken, the market moves rapidly with the trend. However, at times after crossing a trend line, the market pulls back to touch the trend line and then moves in the direction of the trend.

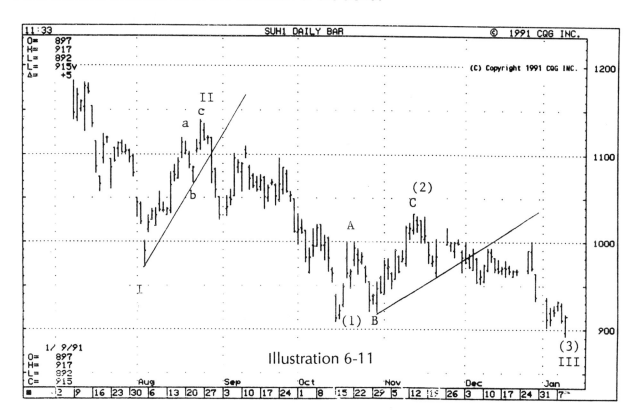

Illustration 6-11

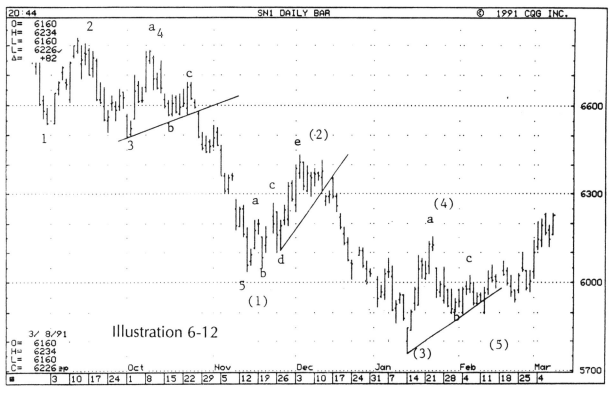

Illustration 6-12

79

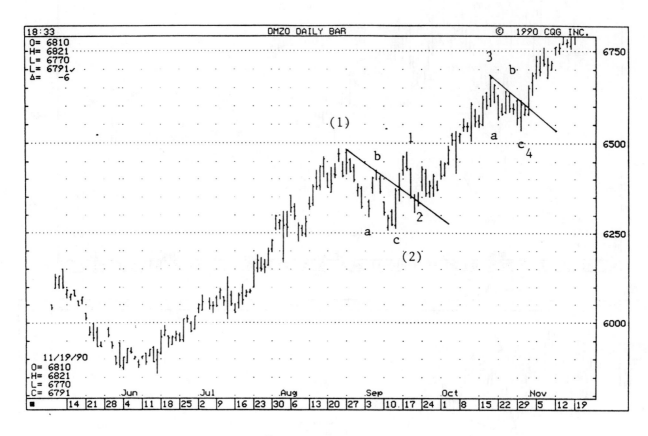

Illustration 6-13

CHAPTER SEVEN

Profit Targets, Protective Stops And Money Management

In setting profit targets and protective stops with Symmetry Wave, my experience has been to lean towards levels on the higher end while avoiding the extremes. The range of feasible levels runs on a curve (for both targets and stops) with the optimal level found toward the higher end of the mid-range. With so many different markets and ever-changing market conditions, there can obviously be no one ideal level for either stops or targets. However, I do have my preferences as to how to handle establishing these critical parameters. More often than not, I find myself using the market's ATR as a base and guide for setting these levels. More on ATR momentarily.

PROTECTIVE STOPS

Generally, with Symmetry Wave, I've found using smaller stops DOES NOT reduce drawdown. I prefer going with the wider stop, say $1,500 as opposed to $250. With the bigger stop, the number of losing trades decreases substantially, and although the total dollar amount of the losses remain about the same, there are more winning trades and the net profit will go up. Here are typical results when using smaller stops versus bigger stops with Symmetry Wave.

Profit Target ➡ Protective Stop ➡	$1,000 $300		$1,000 $600		$1,000 $1,500	
	35 winners	$35,000	44 winners	$44,000	56 winners	$56,000
	50 losses	$15,000	29 losses	$17,400	16 losses	$22,500
	Net	+$20,000	Net	+$26,600	Net	+$33,500

Note that the following conclusions can either be derived directly, or safely assumed, from this one table:

1. The maximum drawdown is increased, not decreased, when too small a protective stop is used.
2. The smaller protective stops cause more frequent losses, and greater strings of losses.

3. By using smaller protective stops, some profitable trades are missed. Therefore, the net profit is less.
4. The larger protective stops have the same drawdown as the smaller stops.
5. By using larger stops, there will be more winning trades.

PROFIT TARGETS

My experience with setting profit targets has led to conclusions similar to those reached with stops. Bigger, but not too big, is better. Even though bigger profit targets are reached less often, they produce greater net profits. Though this is true in general, I've found it particularly to be the case with Symmetry Wave trading. Here are typical results when altering the target level.

Profit Target ➡	$500		$750		$1,500	
Protective Stop ➡	$500		$500		$500	
	85 winners	$42,500	77 winners	$57,750	48 winners	$72,000
	42 losers	$21,000	42 losers	$21,000	42 losers	$21,000
	Net	$21,500	Net	$36,750	Net	$51,000

Clearly, the smaller profit target generates a smaller net profit, even though there are more winners. When a $250 profit target was used (not shown) in order to increase the number of winning trades, the net profit fell down even further to $11,500.

On the other hand, going for too large a profit target (for example, $3,000 in Soybeans or $6,000 in T-Bonds) will reduce the number of winners as well as total profit. This whole basic concept of a Profit Curve to select the ideal target level is illustrated in a simple manner below. Please realize the same concept applies to the choice of stops, although not shown here.

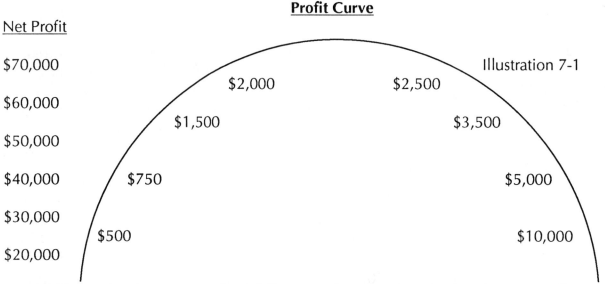

Profit Curve

This illustration demonstrates how different profit targets from $500 to $10,000 will generate different net profits. The scale on the left is the net profit amount and the numbers in the arc represent the amount of the profit target per trade. The smaller and bigger profit targets resulted in the least amount of profit, whereas the mid-range profit targets produced the most profit in the long run.

A $500 profit target resulted in about a $30,000 net profit, whereas a $2,000 profit target resulted in twice as much profit. In contrast, going for too big a profit target (i.e. - $10,000) resulted in the least amount of profit.

So, as stated earlier, there is no one universal ideal profit target. While smaller profit targets generate more winning trades, bigger profit targets generate more profit. However, do avoid the extremes. Too small or too big a profit target will not generate adequate profit.

USING AVERAGE TRUE RANGE FOR STOPS AND TARGETS

ATR gives us the current volatility of each market and becomes a benchmark from which the protective stop and profit target can be calculated. Of course, as with dollar amounts, a profit target of "one times the ATR" will be reached more often than a profit target of "three times the ATR;" however, the larger profit target will yield a greater net profit. Based on ten years of research, my suggestion is to use a *minimum* of about "one and one-half ATR" as a protective stop *and* as a profit target.

I prefer using ATR because it links the size of both my stops and targets to recent activity in the markets. For real-time trading, it is not wise to use arbitrarily selected "dollar figure" amounts because each market has its unique contract size and degree of volatility. For example, the ATR in Bonds might be $800, while the ATR for Corn is $175. This means that if you choose to use "one ATR" for the protective stop and "twice the ATR" for the profit target, then the protective stop for Treasury Bonds would be $800 and the protective stop for corn would be $175. The profit target would be $1,600 for Treasury Bonds and $350 for corn. Each parameter level selected is then in step with current conditions in the particular market being traded.

Following are some recent test results based on seven months of Symmetry Wave trading on eleven markets. The test used ATR levels and again shows how it is easier to earn money with reasonably bigger targets and stop levels.

Profit Target	3 ATR	1.50 ATR	1.50 ATR
Protective Stop	3 ATR	1.50 ATR	1/2 ATR (very small stop)
Move stop to break-even after market moves	1/2 ATR	1/2 ATR	1/2 ATR
Profitable Trades	31	45	25
Losing Trades	12	20	32
Break-Even Trades	39	25	12
Net Profit	$19,000	$12,500	$4,500

(Please note that this same principle of using the ATR applies to stock market trading also.)

To further illustrate how different-sized protective stops and profit targets affect the net results, a Corn chart (Illustration 7-2) and the following combination of parameters will be used:

	Protective Stop	Profit Target
First Parameter	1.0 x ATR	1.5 x ATR
Second Parameter	2.0 x ATR	2.0 x ATR
Third Parameter	2.0 x ATR	4.0 x ATR

The rules for trading are as follows:

1. Only the retracements that are at least one ATR and greater will be used. Retracements that are smaller than one ATR are ignored.
2. Protective stops will not be moved to neutral after price moves in our favor (something I often do in my trading).
3. Protective stops and profit targets will be as indicated.
4. Entry price is 90% of the previous reciprocal Symmetry Wave.
5. To calculate the ATR the most recent 10 days are used. As price fluctuates, ATR expands and contracts based on current volatility.
6. Since Corn is not very volatile, two contracts are traded.

CORN

Trade No.	ATR (in dollars)	Profit 1.5 ATR Stop 1 ATR	Profit 2.0 ATR Stop 2.0 ATR	Profit 4.0 ATR Stop 2.0 ATR
1	$450	$ - 450	$ + 900	$ + 1,800
2	$450	+ 675	+ 900	+ 1,800
3	$300	- 300	- 600	- 600
4	$300	- 300	+ 600	+ 1,200
5	$300	+ 450	+ 600	+ 1,200
6	$400	+ 600	+ 800	+ 1,600
7	$300	+ 450	+ 600	+ 1,200
8	$250	+ 375	+ 500	- 250
9	$300	- 300	Open	No trade*
10	$300	+ 450	+ 600	Open
Winners:		6 at $3,000	8 at $5,500	6 at $8,800
Losers:		4 at -1,350	1 at -600	2 at -850
Net:		+ 1,650	+ 4,900	+ 7,950

No trade because trade number 8 and 9 are at a similar price, and trade number 8 has not earned a profit yet.

As can be seen here again, choosing too small of a protective stop and profit target is not the way to go. By using a bigger protective stop, the number of losing trades was reduced, and by

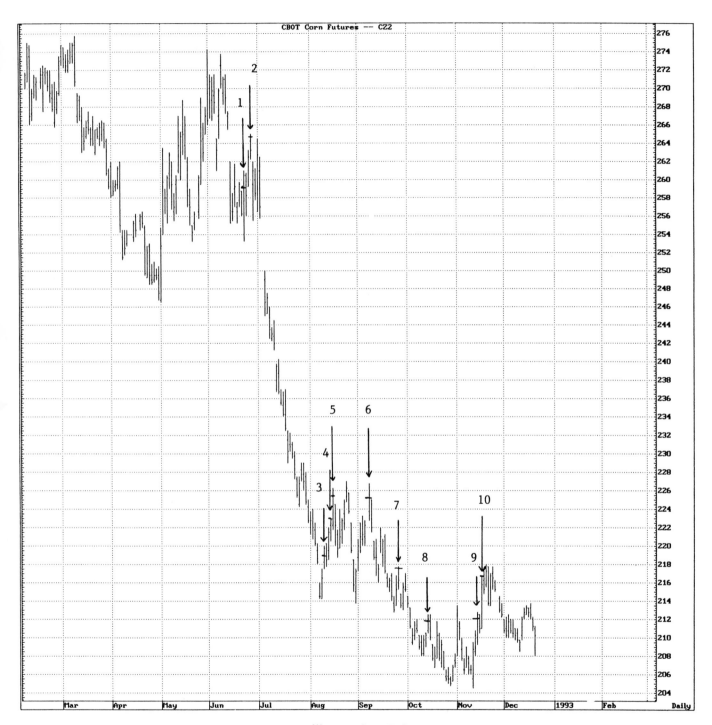

Illustration 7-2

trading for bigger profits, the net earnings double or triple. However, your decision on stop and target parameters should not be guided by profits alone, but also by your personality. For some people, it is easier to take quicker profits, while others are more comfortable staying in a while longer and targeting bigger profits. I, personally, never use less than a "one and one-half ATR" profit target. Below that level, profits are often too small to compensate for commissions, slippage and errors. My recommendation to you would be to consider following that same rule of thumb.

And always keep in mind that sequence of entry is very important. Enter the market the first time you set your trading signal. The best trades usually do not give you a second chance. Also, if you wait to act on your signal, you often find yourself missing out on a chunk of profit that could have been locked in by establishing a break-even stop at the time of the initial signal.

MONEY MANAGEMENT TOPICS

Pyramiding

Pyramiding can be used for adding more positions in the same market without increasing the risk of losing. If you feel a market is in a very strong trend and instead of diversifying into other markets you wish to add more positions in the same market (without exposing your account to unnecessary risk), then pyramiding is a viable solution. This is true provided, that is, that you only add positions in the same amount that you started with and in such a way that if the market goes against you, you will not lose more than the equivalent of your first protective stop. For example, if your protective stop is $500, and the market moves $500 in your favor, you could add another position and move the protective stop for the first trade up to break-even. Then, if the market goes against you, you will be risking only $500.

If you start with one contract, and the market moves in your favor, and then you add two more contracts (and as the market moves in your favor you add a greater amount of contracts) you will expose your account to a substantial risk of losing a large sum of money should even a small price fluctuation go against your positions.

BREAK-EVEN STOPS

Moving the protective stop to break-even when a trade is ahead is a good strategy for reducing the number of losing trades and the drawdown; however, the winning trades are also reduced. Therefore, in general, the net profit remains about the same as if you had *not* used a break-even stop. Following are typical differing results obtained by using break-even stops and *not* using break-even stops.

Without Break-Even Stops	With Break-Even Stops
30 winning trades	25 winning trades
20 losing trades	12 losing trades
	13 break-even
50 total trades	50 total trades

With break-even stops, the accuracy is higher due to fewer losses, but the net profit remains about the same. Also, with break-even stops in place, the ratio of winners to losers improves and greater confidence is created. On the other hand, using break-even stops could require monitoring of the market throughout the trading day, creating more stress. Personally, even though I have not found it to be advantageous to use break-even stops with other trading systems, it is beneficial to use break-even stops with Symmetry Wave. I use break-even stops with Symmetry Wave by waiting for the market to move about three-fourths ATR in my favor from the entry price; then I move the protective stop to the break-even price. *This strategy of moving the protective stop to the break-even price does reduce the drawdown.*

TRADING DIFFERENT TIME FRAMES

Whether you are trading daily bar charts, five-minute bars or weekly charts, the same guidelines for protective stops and profit targets apply. Use the recent 10-bar ATR to determine the current volatility and to calculate the protective stop and profit target.

However, also never rule out good old-fashioned experience in helping you select protective stops and profit targets. For example, I found a 100 point move in the S&P 500 (when using five-minute bar charts) to be superior to other targets, and I adjusted my trading accordingly.

DIVERSIFICATION

The idea underlying the concept of diversification is that if several markets are traded, then the size of the portfolio's drawdown will be reduced. The reasoning here is that if four or five positions are losing money, then at least two or three positions should be making money, thereby effectively reducing the potential drawdown. Also implied in the concept of diversification is the idea that since the potential drawdown is reduced, more markets can be traded with the same amount of money.

A number of years ago, I did a small "diversification test." I took a portfolio of five markets, and a portfolio of three different markets, monitored them for a period of months, then graphed the results. It was interesting to see the inescapable conclusion I had already drawn depicted visually. Diversification did not reduce the potential drawdown but it did increase the drawdown (as well as the profits). The fluctuation between profits and losses became more volatile despite diversifying among unrelated markets.

Here is the graphic demonstration of those test results:

Portfolio One: Soybeans, Deutsche Mark, Crude Oil, T-Bonds, Sugar. *(Indicated by small dash line.)*

Portfolio Two: New York Composite, Coffee, Cotton. *(Indicated by large dash line.)*

Combined Portfolios: *(Indicated by solid line.)*

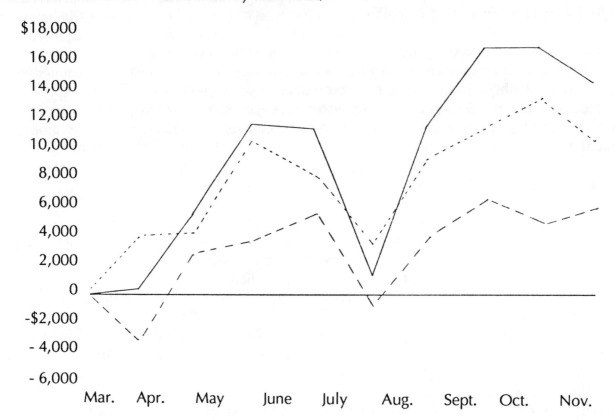

The worst drawdown of Portfolio One was $6,000.00, the worst drawdown of Portfolio Two was $5,000.00, whereas the worst drawdown of the Combined Portfolio was $10,000.00. The largest gain in Portfolio One was $10,000. Portfolio Two's biggest gain was $9,000.00. Meanwhile, the Combined Portfolio achieved a biggest gain of $15,000.00. There was only one flat (neutral) month in Portfolio One, in Portfolio Two there were no flat months; whereas when the two portfolios were combined, there were three flat months.

To sum it up, diversification did not reduce the size of the potential drawdown, but it did reduce the frequency of the losing months as well as the frequency of the winning months, thus effectively increasing the number of flat months. Overall profits were higher. This type of performance has been typical of Symmetry Wave portfolio behavior as well.

The main reason that diversification did not and does not behave with every trading system exactly as the "laws of mathematics" would seem to dictate, is due to the fact that often all markets enter into a sideways pattern or reverse their trend within the same short time frame, thus causing all or many markets to lose (temporarily) at the same time. Since diversifying among many markets does not reduce the size of the drawdowns, *more capital is needed for each additional market that is traded in a portfolio.*

Futures magazine, in their August 1991 issue, wrote an article titled "Specialized Traders Go Against the Grain of Diversification." The specialized traders, in other words, those traders that concentrate on specific markets such as currencies or petroleum products, have outperformed the traders who diversify among many markets. In a separate instance, a well-established managed futures fund, on their diversified account, had an annual return of about 22% and a largest drawdown of about 28%, whereas their currency program had an annual return of about 37% and a worst drawdown of about 19%.

The reason for the better success of specialized trading is mainly due to the fact that it is easier to find a trading system that works for a specific type of market. Each market's behavior is different. Crude Oil, Eurodollars, and Deutsche Marks are strong trending markets; therefore, trend-oriented trading systems work well with these markets. Live cattle, wheat, and sugar, on the other hand, are choppier and experience more sideways markets; therefore, a trading system designed to take advantage of a strong trend will not do as well in these markets.

My last word on diversification is a quote from Albert Einstein, which helps understand why many systems have somewhat contrary experiences with diversification (at least as it applies to drawdowns) in real-time trading:

"As far as the laws of mathematics refer to reality, they are not certain; and as far as they are certain, they do not refer to reality."

METHOD SUMMARY

Following is a brief summarization of what I believe to be the best way to use the Symmetry Wave Trading Method:

1. Only trade with the major trend (see Chapter 4).

2. Calculate the size of the previous retracement wave you wish to trade from (see Chapter 3).

3. When the market retraces 90% of the previous wave you are trading from, enter the market.

4. Consider using a protective stop of two times the 10-day ATR (see Chapter 7).

5. Consider using a profit target of three times the 10-day ATR (see Chapter 7).

6. When a trade is ahead by 3/4 of the 10-day ATR, move the protective stop to about a $50 profit to compensate for commissions and slippage (see Chapter 7).

7. Execute quickly (I put all my orders in before the markets open).

8. Keep on trading after a drawdown period in order to recover losses and earn a profit.

9. Don't put on too many positions in relation to your trading account size.

SECTION 3

Related Symmetry Wave Topics

CHAPTER EIGHT

Stocks

Since both the stock and futures markets are influenced by human nature, as well as world and economic events, their patterns of behavior are somewhat repetitive. Symmetry Wave will identify and capture a specific repetitive pattern equally well in both types of markets. The first pattern in each type of market is the retracement wave 2, with the repetitive patterns being retracement waves 4, 6, and possibly wave 8 (see Chapter Three).

A misconception the public holds is that the futures markets are more volatile than stock markets. In reality, the stock market has become more volatile in recent years. The reason futures appear to be more volatile is that they are highly leveraged. Stock markets can only be leveraged up to 50%, whereas futures are leveraged up to 95%. If the volatility of stocks was compared to commodities without any leverage, then stocks are more volatile. You won't see a bushel of corn go from $3.00 to $1.00, but in stocks you will see a market rapidly drop from $12.00 to $2.00.

Symmetry Wave provides a window of opportunity to enter the markets at an ideal support or resistance range. You may choose to enter the markets when the Symmetry Wave is reached, or wait for some indicator, price pattern, or significant news item to confirm your entry into the markets.

In this chapter I give examples of different Symmetry Wave counts and entries on weekly stock charts. The same rules are used here for the stock charts as were used for the futures charts in Chapters three through seven. You'll notice not all waves are counted. The reason being I stayed with the bigger Symmetry Wave count as much as possible. Only for illustration purposes do I, on occasion, count the smaller Symmetry Waves. Another reason for not counting a wave is when a retracement wave does not have a matching symmetrical retracement wave. In these instances it is not necessary to mark the wave. You then wait for the next set of Symmetry Waves to develop, or wait until a previous wave is matched symmetrically. Remember, the count for a symmetrical wave stops if there is not a matching retracement wave. See illustrations 8-5 and 8-6.

The following pages contain a number of charts. The idea here is to illustrate, as much as possible, the proper Symmetry Wave count so your eyes get trained to see groups of symmetrical sets of waves. It is important to count all of the symmetrical waves within the same group. That is to say, it is all right not to count a certain set of Symmetry Waves if you do not wish to trade off of that set, but once a count has started for a certain magnitude of waves, all the waves of the same magnitude that fall in that set must be accounted for.

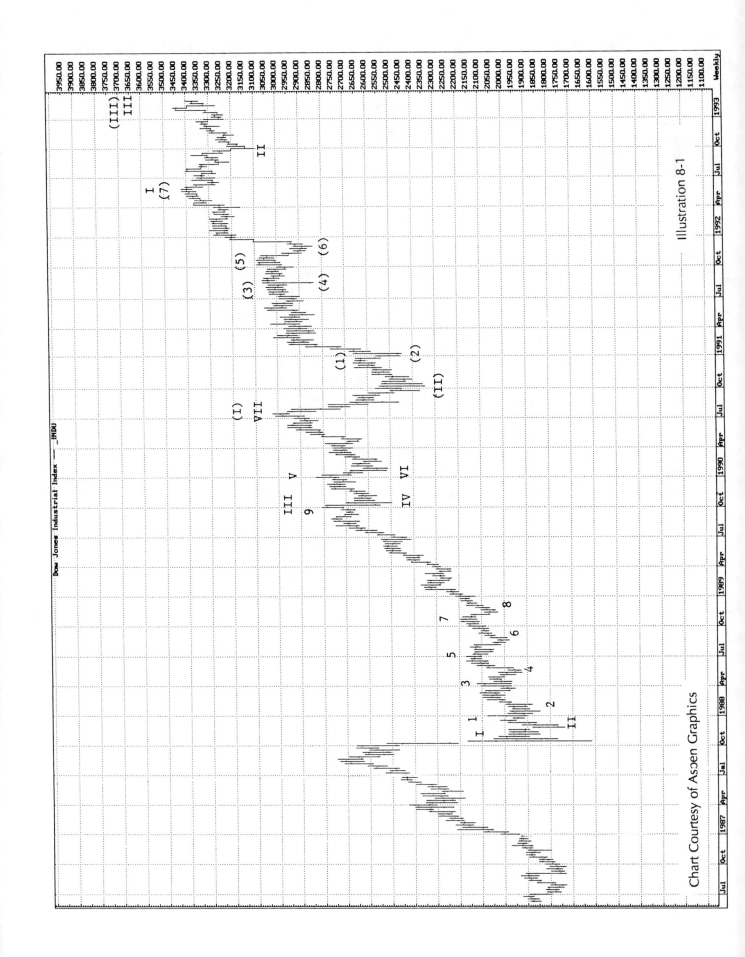

Dow Jones Industrial Index — _INDU

Chart Courtesy of Aspen Graphics

Illustration 8-1

AMGEN

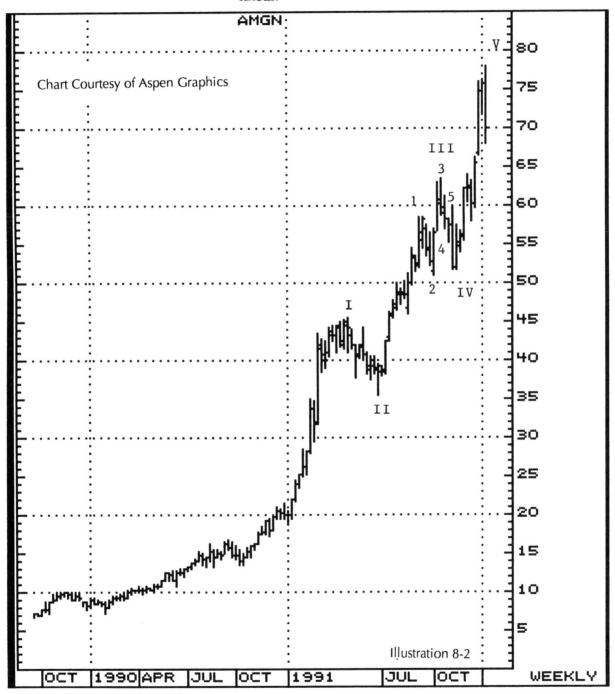

Illustration 8-2

93

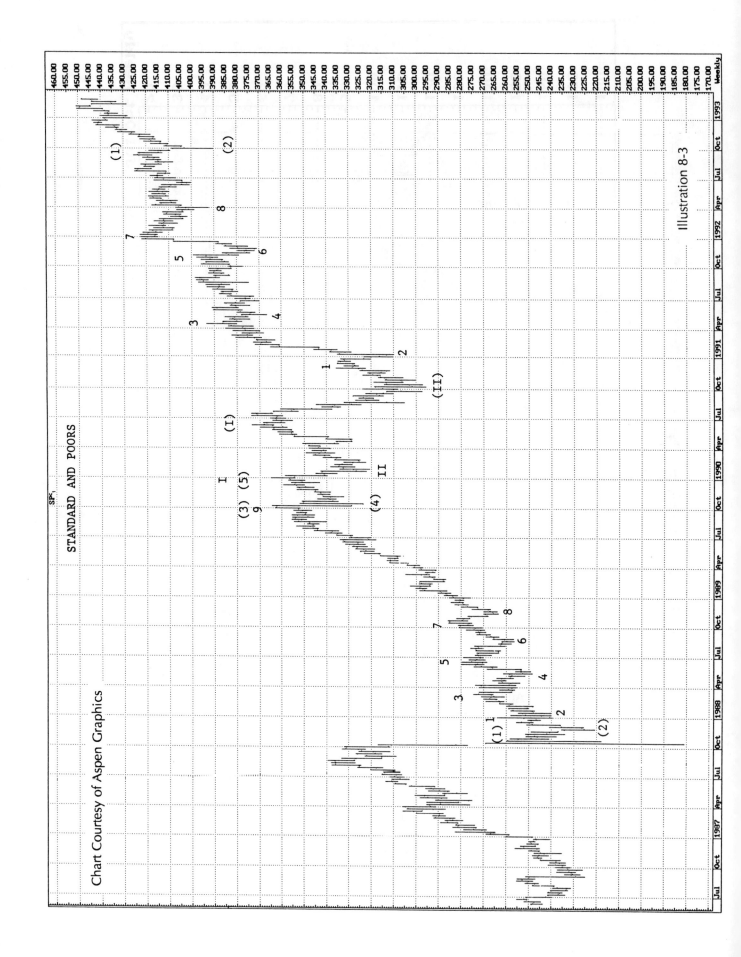

STANDARD AND POORS

Chart Courtesy of Aspen Graphics

Illustration 8-3

94

ATLANTIC RICHFIELD

ARC

Chart Courtesy of Aspen Graphics

Illustration 8-4

95

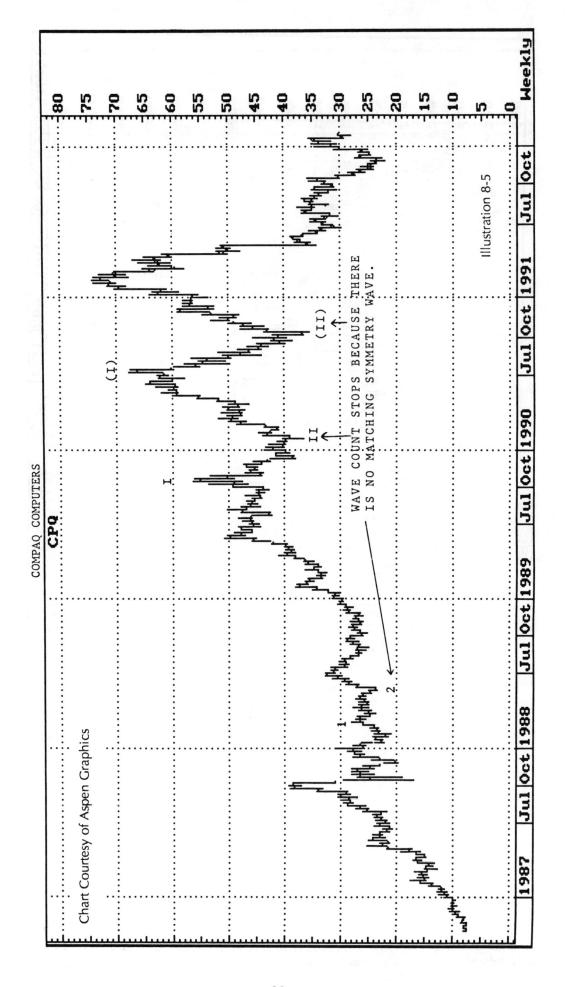

COMPAQ COMPUTERS

CPQ

Chart Courtesy of Aspen Graphics

WAVE COUNT STOPS BECAUSE THERE
IS NO MATCHING SYMMETRY WAVE.

Illustration 8-5

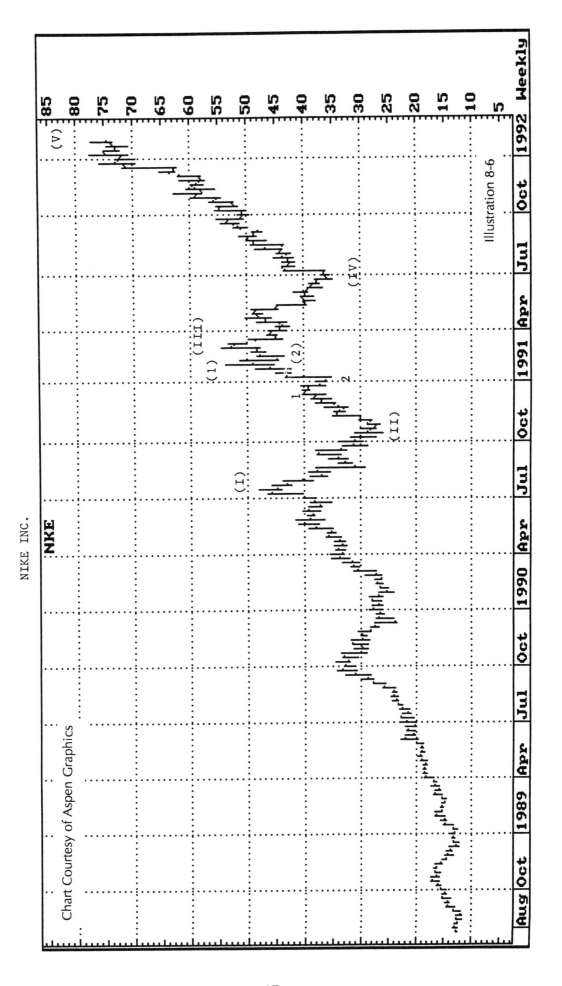

NIKE INC.

NKE

Chart Courtesy of Aspen Graphics

Illustration 8-6

97

NOVELL INC.

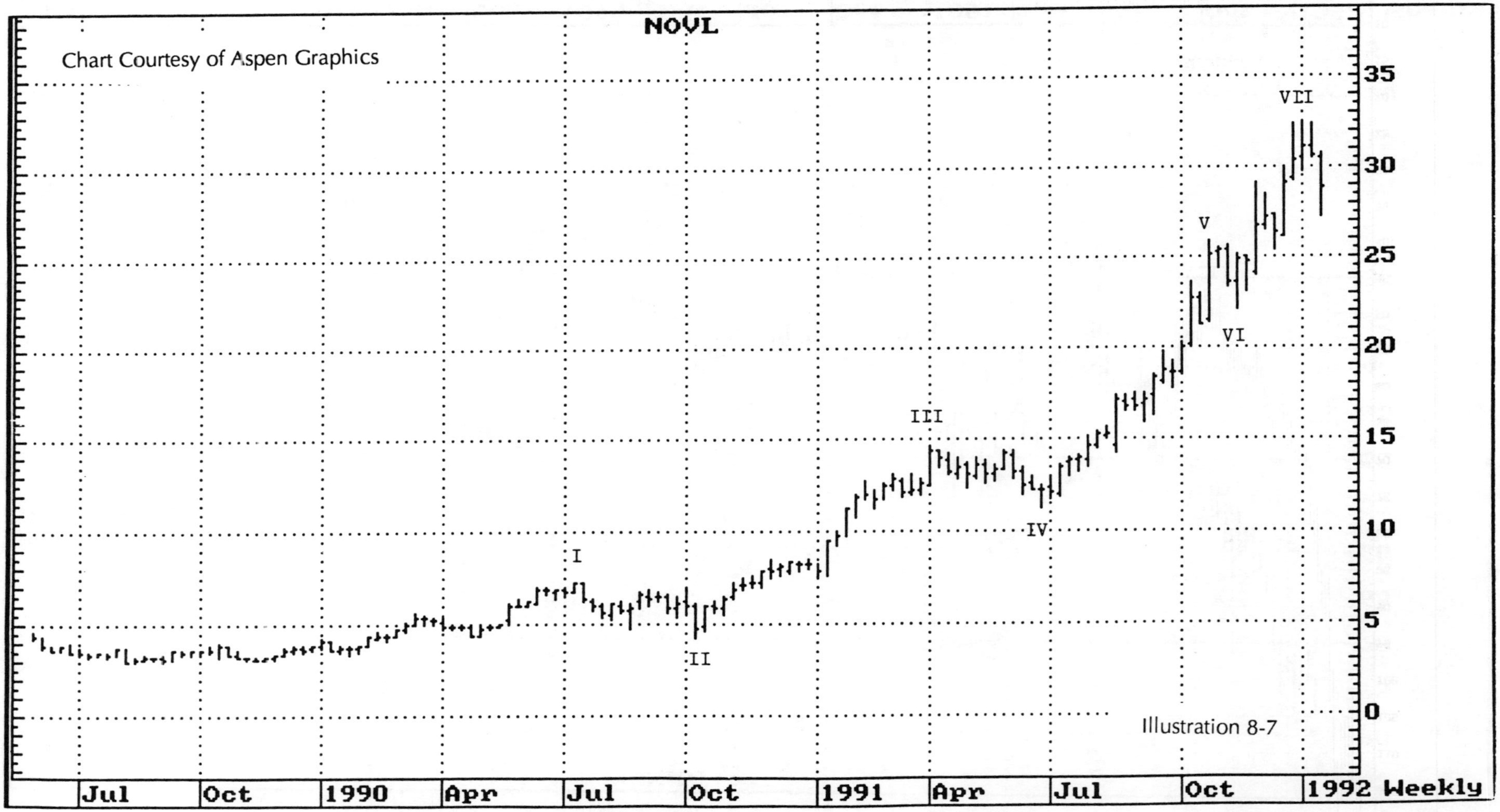
NOVL
Chart Courtesy of Aspen Graphics
35
30
25
20
15
10
5
0
I
II
III
IV
V
VI
VII
Jul
Oct
1990
Apr
Jul
Oct
1991
Apr
Jul
Oct
1992 Weekly

Illustration 8-7

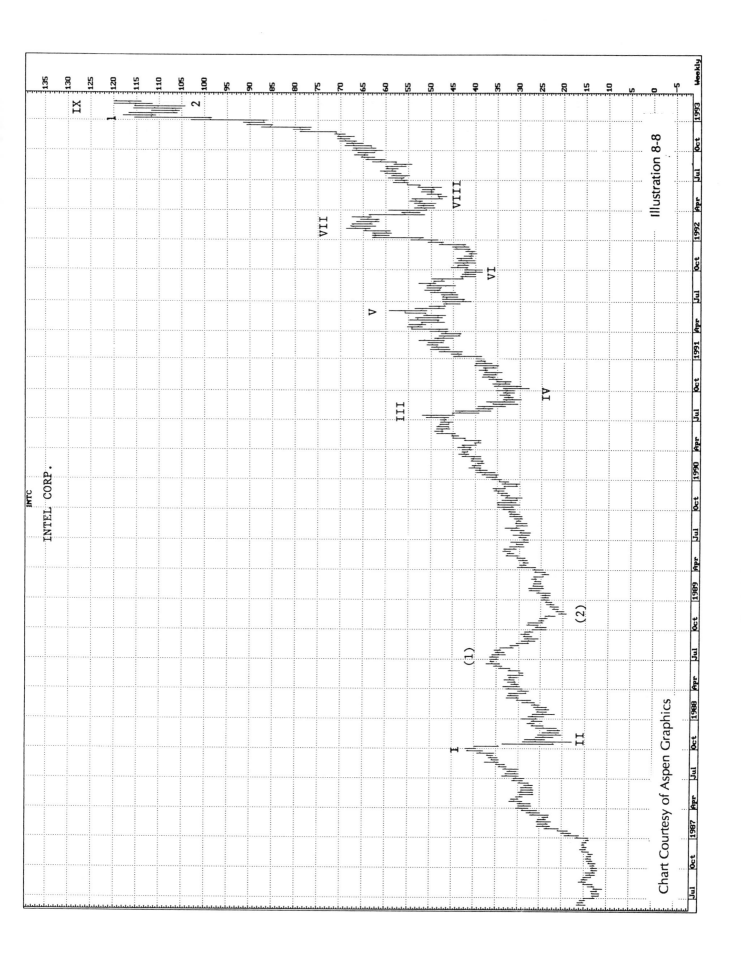

INTEL CORP.

Chart Courtesy of Aspen Graphics

Illustration 8-8

PHILLIP MORRIS

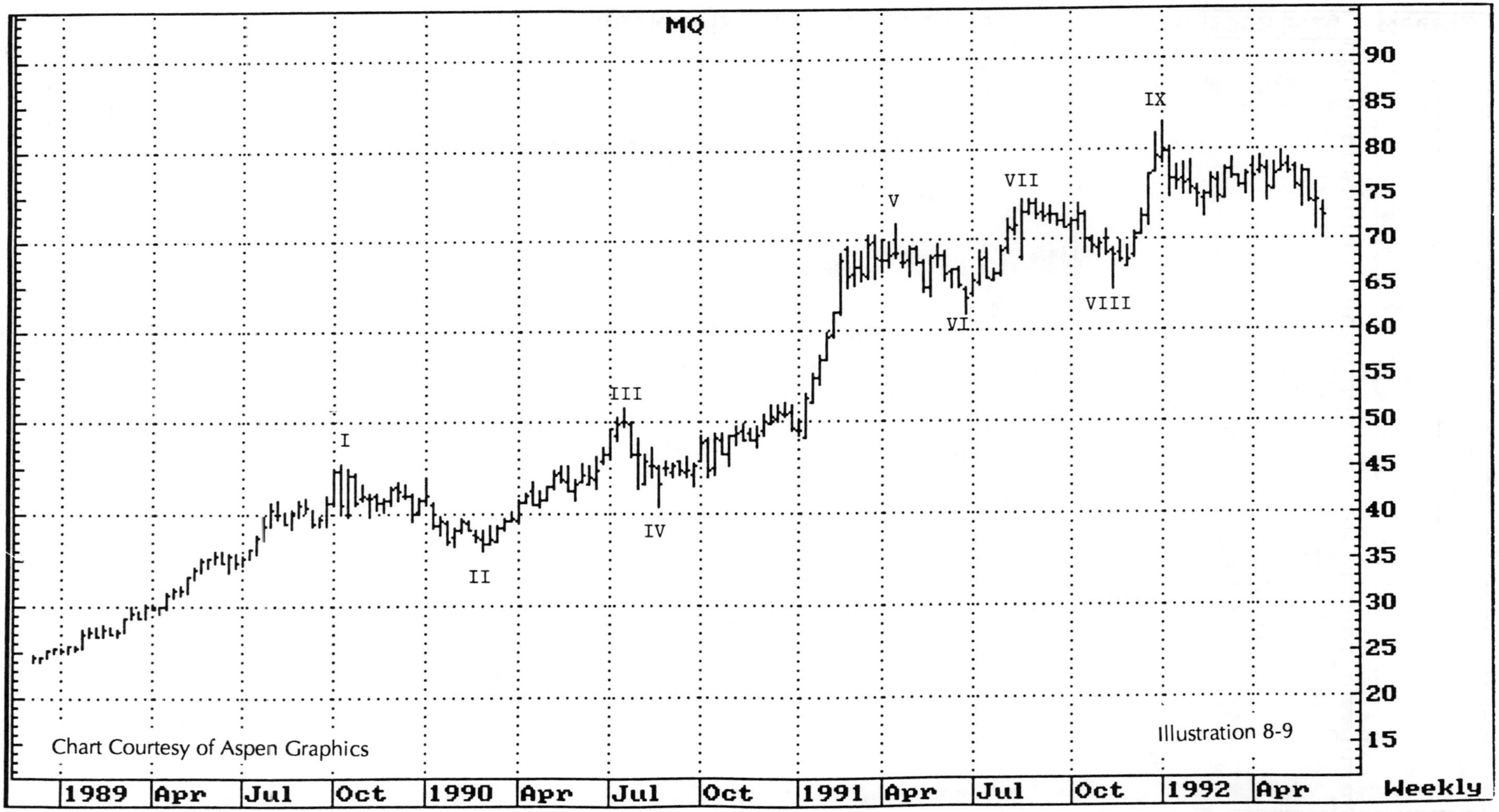

MQ
90
85
80
75
70
65
60
55
50
45
40
35
30
25
20
15
I
II
III
IV
V
VI
VII
VIII
IX
1989
Apr
Jul
Oct
1990
Apr
Jul
Oct
1991
Apr
Jul
Oct
1992
Apr
Weekly
Chart Courtesy of Aspen Graphics
Illustration 8-9

SARA LEE CORPORATION

SLE

Chart Courtesy of Aspen Graphics

Illustration 8-10

101

CHAPTER NINE

Day Trading

Day trading, though potentially very rewarding, is probably the most difficult way to trade. It is rewarding because you know the results of your trading sooner than in longer-term trading. No trades are exposed to overnight events, so in theory at least, there should be less stress. Your money is not tied up in margins and drawdown. With day trading, if you lose money today it's possible to recover it tomorrow. However, day trading can be more difficult than long-term trading since, for the most part, you have to be glued to the screen in order not to miss trades. With longer term trading, obviously, there is more time to plan a trade and execute it. Also, for many people day trading is more stressful because they let their minds be affected by each price fluctuation.

Each time frame (i.e., one-, five-, fifteen-, and sixty-minute bar charts) will give a different perspective of the trend; therefore, your first step in day trading with Symmetry Wave will be to decide which time frame to use. Following are several charts presented to illustrate how each time frame gives a different perspective.

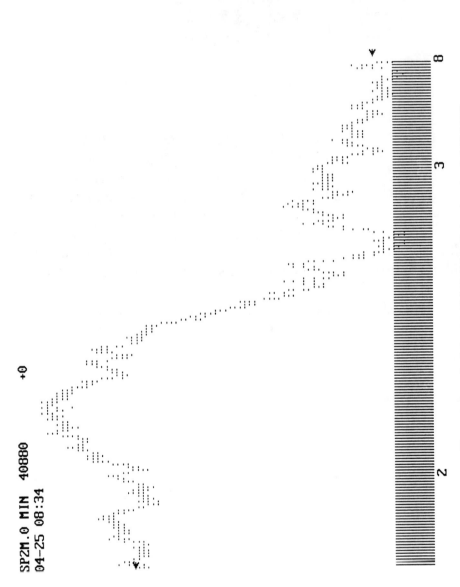

Illustration 9-1 is an S&P 500 tick chart of 4/24/92.

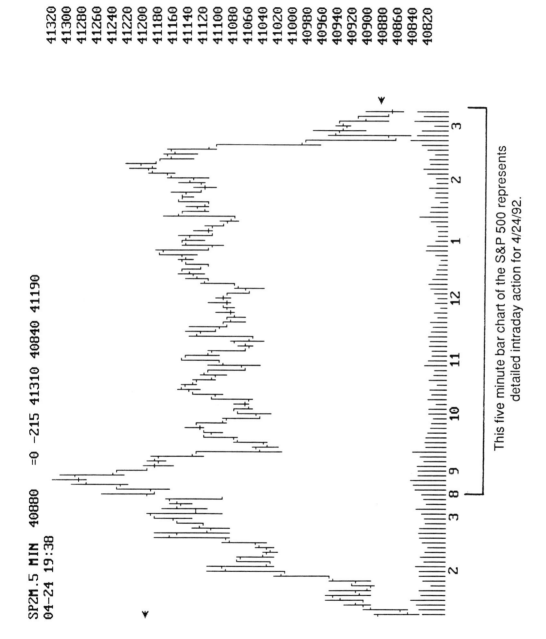

This five minute bar chart of the S&P 500 represents
detailed intraday action for 4/24/92.

Illustration 9-2

SP2M.15 MIN 40880   =0 -215 41310 40840 41190
04-24 19:54

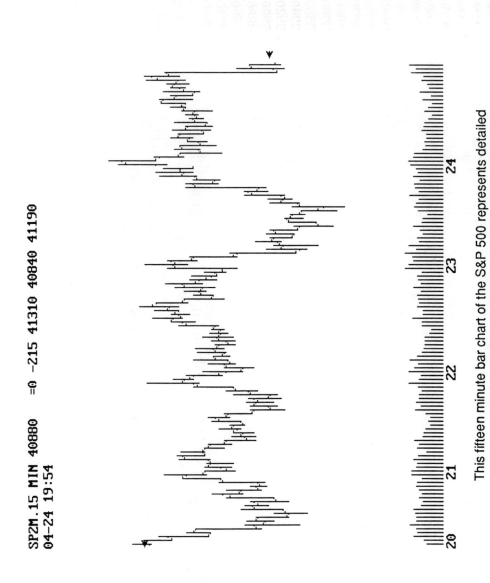

41480
41440
41400
41360
41320
41280
41240
41200
41160
41120
41080
41040
41000
40960
40920
40880
40840
40800
40760
40720
40680
40640
40600
40560
40520
40480

20   21   22   23   24

This fifteen minute bar chart of the S&P 500 represents detailed
intraday price action for 4/24/92. The addition of previous days'
price actions provide a broader perspective of current market conditons.

Illustration 9-3

106

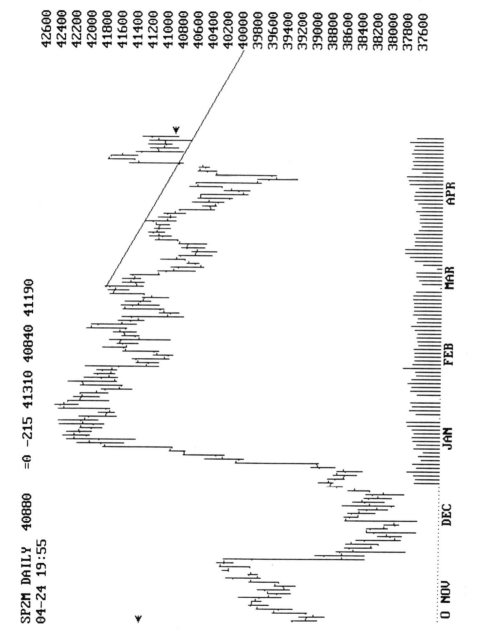

Illustration 9-4 is an S&P 500 daily bar chart of 4/24/92.

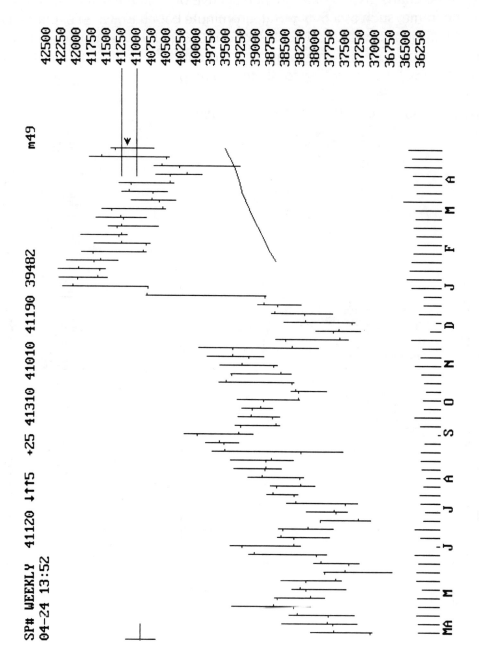

Illustration 9-5 is an S&P 500 weekly bar chart of 4/24/92.

As can be seen from these charts, a daily chart details action of a weekly chart, and a sixty-minute bar chart details the action of a daily chart, and a fifteen-minute bar chart details the action of an hourly chart. This pattern of microcosm within a macrocosm continues down to tick chart level. Thus, inversely, a tick chart expands into a five-minute bar chart, and a five-minute bar chart expands into a daily bar chart, and the progression continues up to the monthly charts.

Each of these charts gives a different perspective of what the market is doing. Furthermore, the same time frame, such as a five- or fifteen-minute bar chart, when expanded or contracted, will give a different perspective. See illustrations 9-6 and 9-7. Because each time frame gives a different perspective, it becomes important to choose one time frame and to stay with it. Otherwise, there will be too many conflicting perceptions and trading signals.

SP2M.15 MIN 40880   =0 -215 41310 40840 41190
04-24 19:54

Illustration 9-6

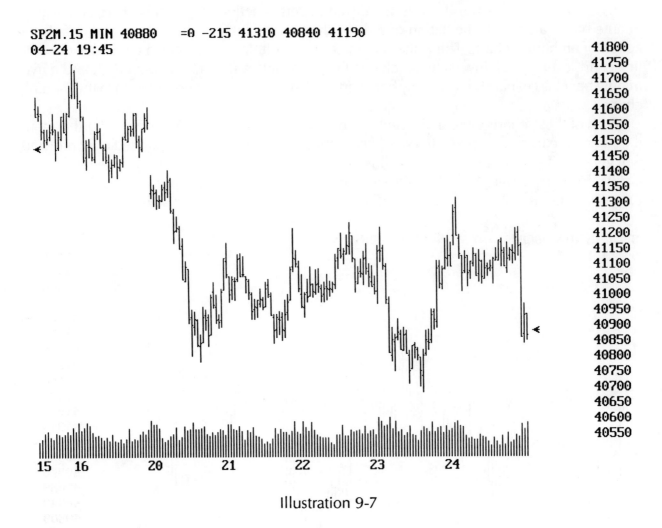

SP2M.15 MIN 40880   =0 -215 41310 40840 41190
04-24 19:45

Illustration 9-7

A bar chart of less than a ten-minute time frame does not give a trader an adequate perspective of the immediate trend, and the shorter time-frame charts, such as a five-minute bar chart, often become too choppy during a sideways market. See illustration 9-8. On the other hand, a sixty-minute bar chart may not yield enough trades to keep your interest. I have found fifteen-minute bar charts to give enough data to get a good idea of the immediate trend, and an adequately large perspective so as not to lose touch with the overall market behavior. At the same time, the fifteen-minute bar chart is responsive enough to catch smaller Symmetry Waves and to generate enough trades to keep even the most avid day traders busy.

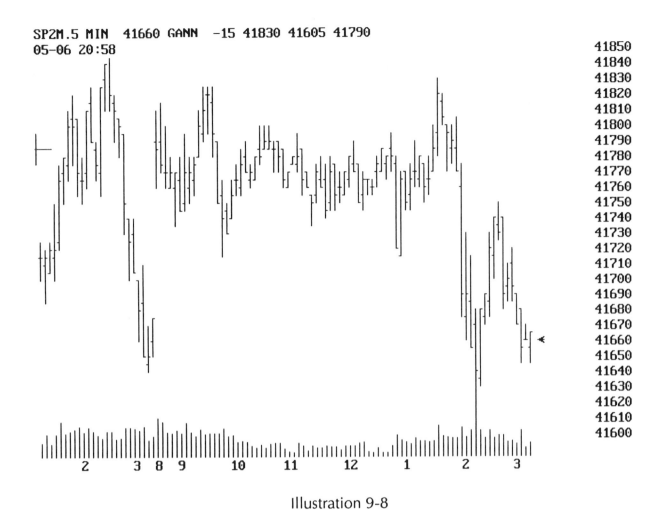

SP2M.5 MIN 41660 GANN -15 41830 41605 41790
05-06 20:58

Illustration 9-8

As these illustrations show, and as I mentioned earlier, the first issue to be resolved with day trading is the time frame to be used, so there won't be conflicting perspectives. One of the ways a conflicting perspective manifests itself is when the fifteen-minute bar chart and the five-minute bar chart give trades in opposite directions. In illustration 9-9, the S&P fifteen-minute bar chart shows the trend to be down, and it has given a sell signal (retracement wave IV), whereas the five-minute bar chart is in an uptrend and is giving a buy signal (retracement wave 4); see illustration 9-10.

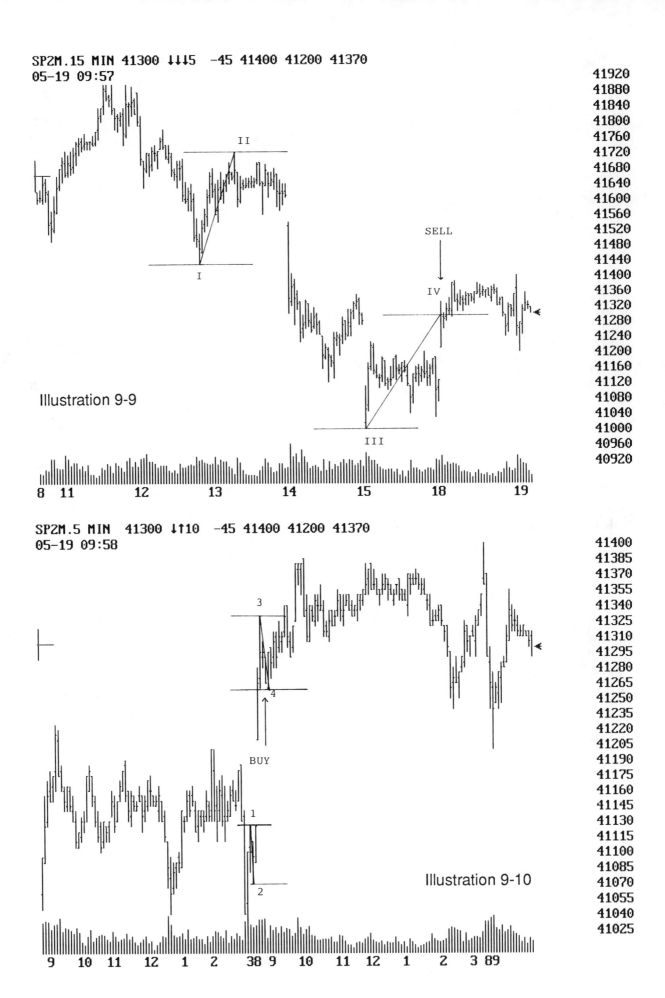

SP2M.15 MIN 41300 ↓↓↓5 -45 41400 41200 41370
05-19 09:57

Illustration 9-9

SP2M.5 MIN 41300 ↓↑10 -45 41400 41200 41370
05-19 09:58

Illustration 9-10

112

The importance of basing day trading on a single time-frame is emphasized for the sake of consistency and clarity of purpose. In the scenario depicted in illustration 9-9, basically there were three choices: (1) to go short using the fifteen-minute Symmetry Wave (wave IV), or (2) to go long using the five-minute Symmetry Wave (wave 4), or (3) to first go short using the fifteen-minute Symmetry Wave and then go long using the five-minute Symmetry Wave. I find it best to use one time frame to trade with. How you choose to trade will depend on your trading style. Whatever you do, try to confine yourself to watching only two time frames at most.

The S&P market, like all markets, has two identifiable phases, sideways markets (or consolidations) and trending markets. See illustration 9-11.

Illustration 9-11

Symmetry Wave works best during the trending markets. One way to gauge the trend of the market is to use the slope of a five- to eight-day moving average (see illustration 9-12). The simplest way is to train your eyes to see when a market is trending and when it is not.

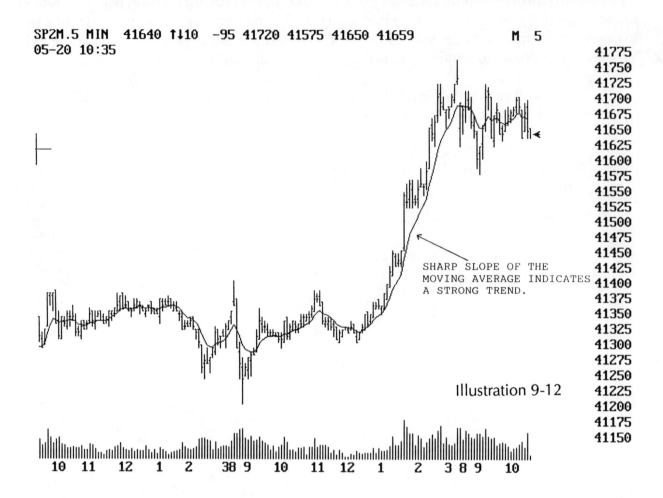

SHARP SLOPE OF THE MOVING AVERAGE INDICATES A STRONG TREND.

Illustration 9-12

To cover the cost of commissions and slippage associated with the execution of trades, it is important to day trade only the most volatile and liquid markets. The favored market of day traders is the S&P 500. All the illustrations in this chapter are in the S&P market.

Other Suggestions And Observations:

- There are few 200-point profits, more 100-point profits, and far more 30-point profits.

- Use wide stops. For example, a 60 point stop-loss is preferable to a 30 point stop-loss. I'm in for a lot more 100 point winners, and that makes a big difference in my final net profit totals.

- To clarify the wave count and to get an overall picture of the market, go back to a bigger time frame.

- It is advisable to day trade only one market. This is because it's not possible to efficiently track two markets within a single day at the same time. Furthermore, each market has its own nuances, and it is important to tune into the specialized nature of a market. By trading more than one market, the nuance of a particular market is lost.

- Trade when the market is in a strong trend.

Incidentally, all charts in this chapter are by Ensign Software. They can be reached at 2641 Shannon Ct., Idaho Falls, ID 83404, Phone: (208) 524-0755.

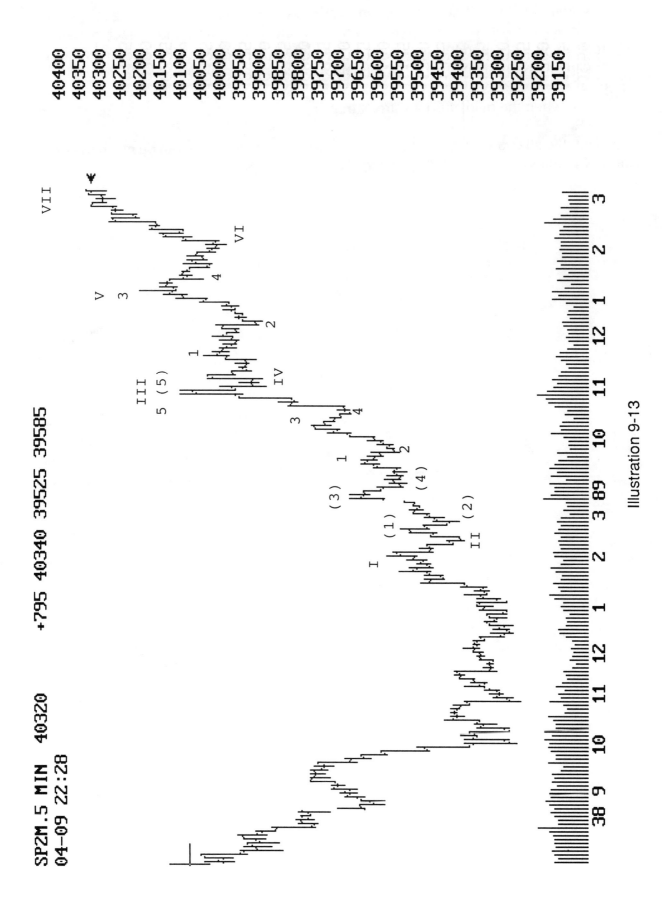

Illustration 9-13

116

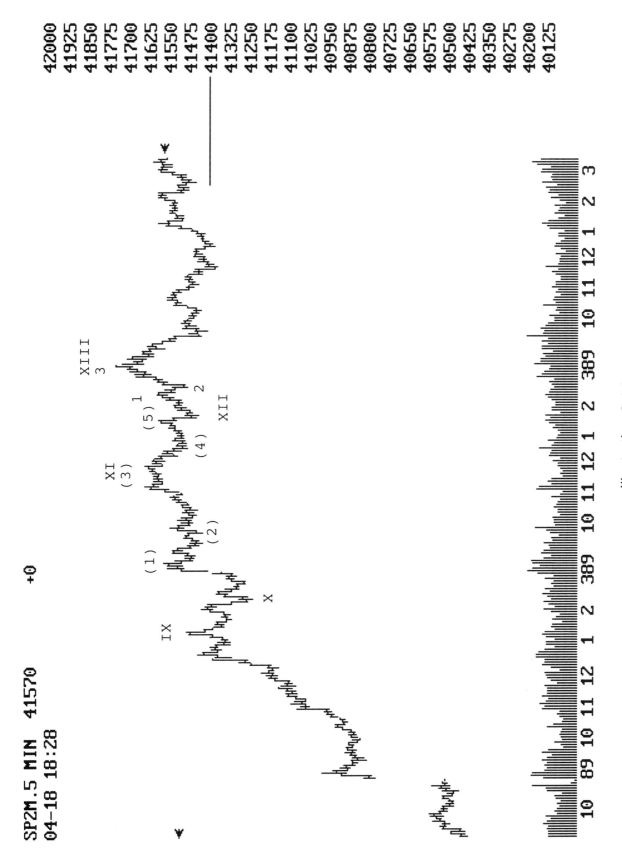

Illustration 9-14

117

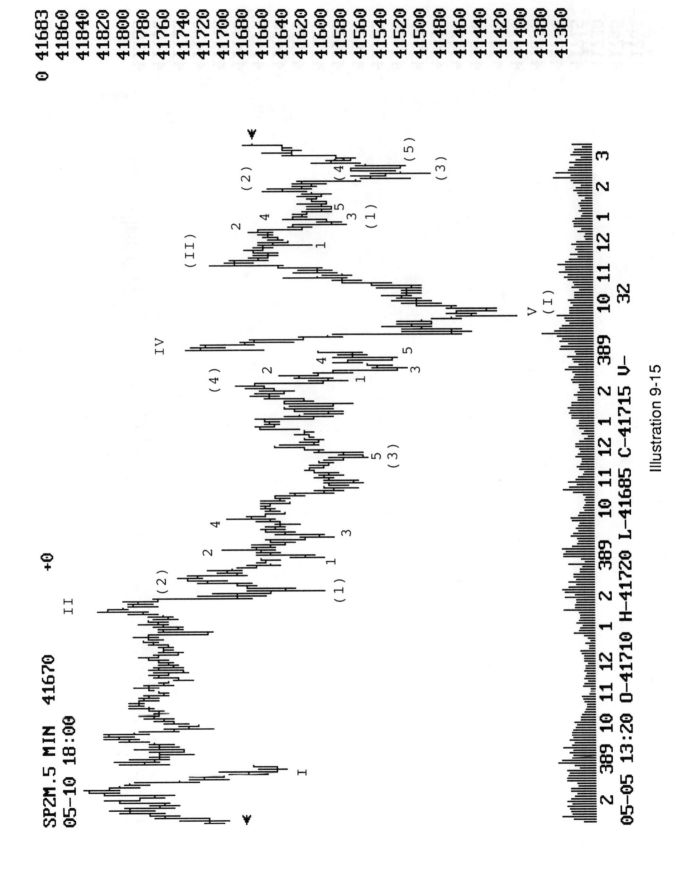

Illustration 9-15

118

Illustration 9-16

119

Illustration 9-17

120

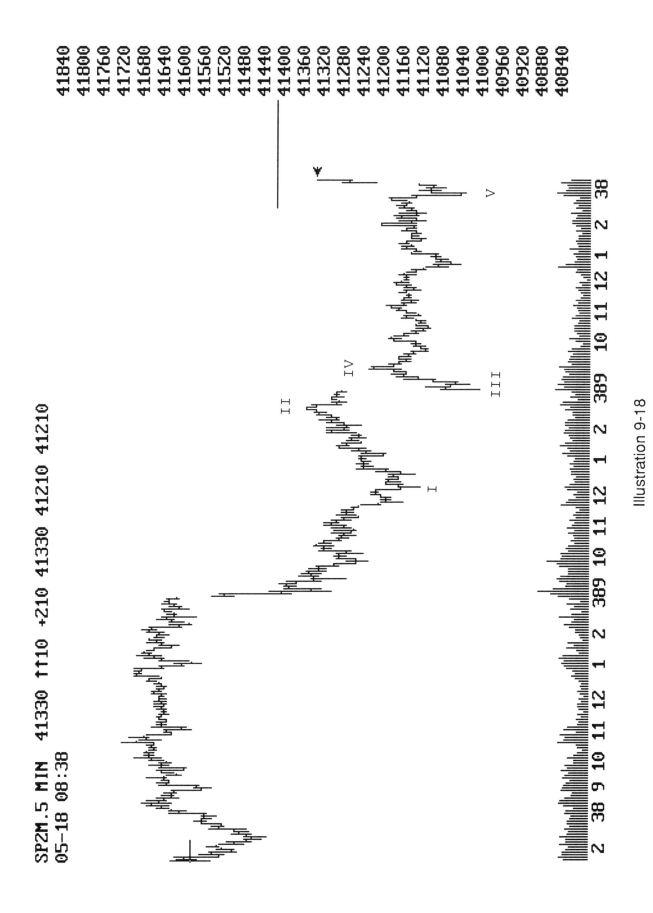

Illustration 9-18

121

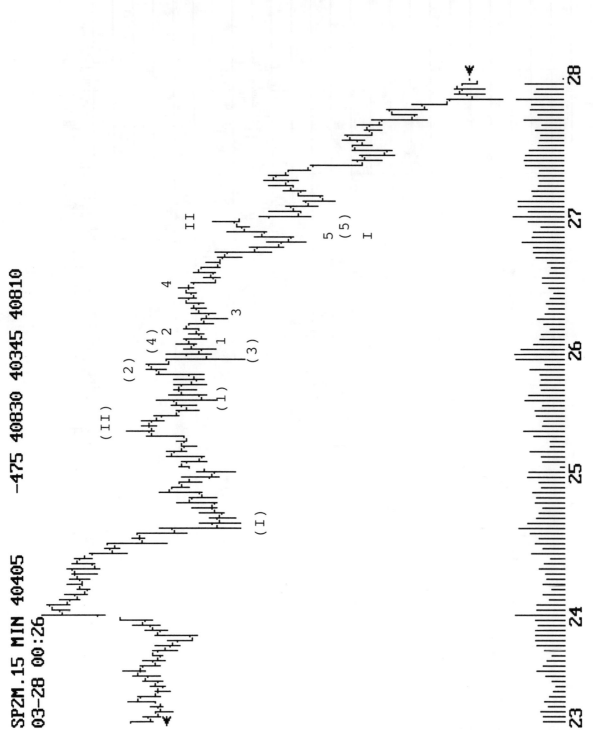

Illustration 9-19

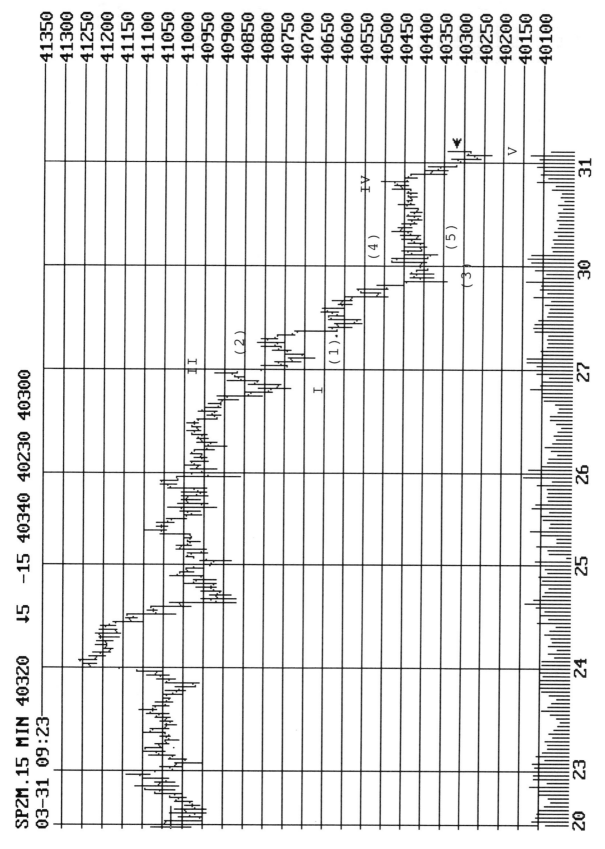

Illustration 9-20

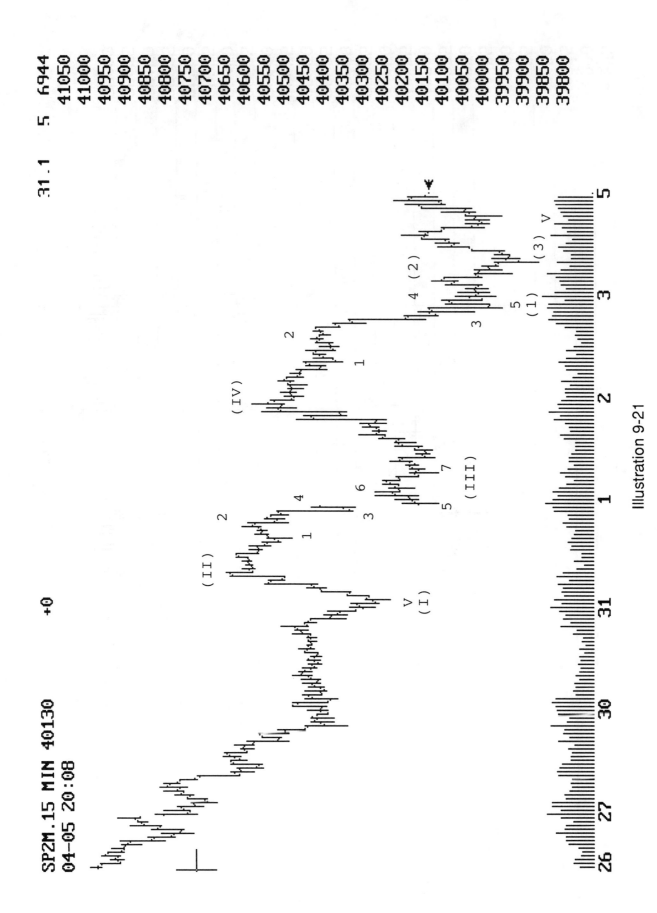

Illustration 9-21

124

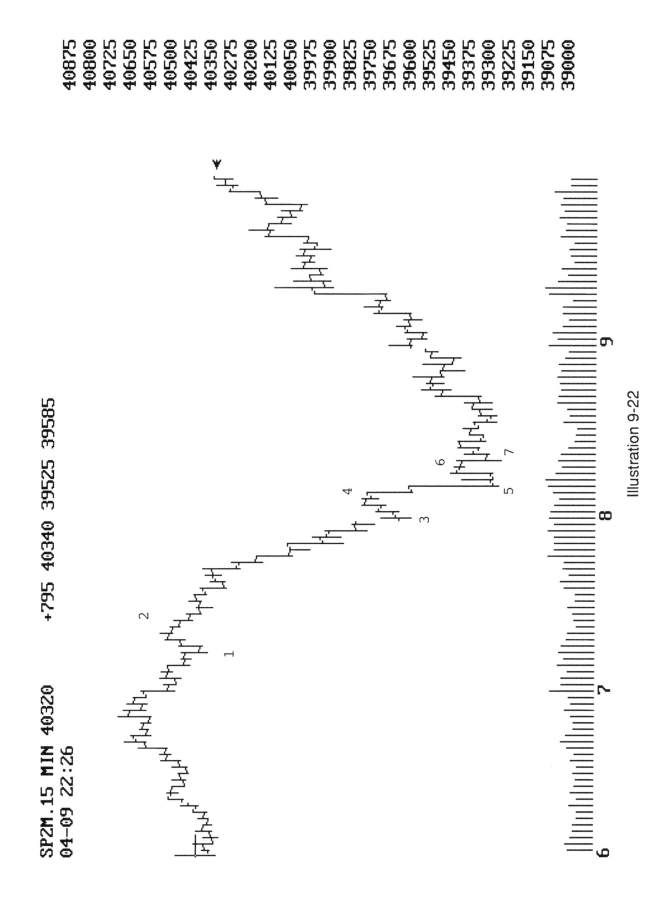

SP2M.15 MIN 40320   +795 40340 39525 39585
04-09 22:26

Illustration 9-22

125

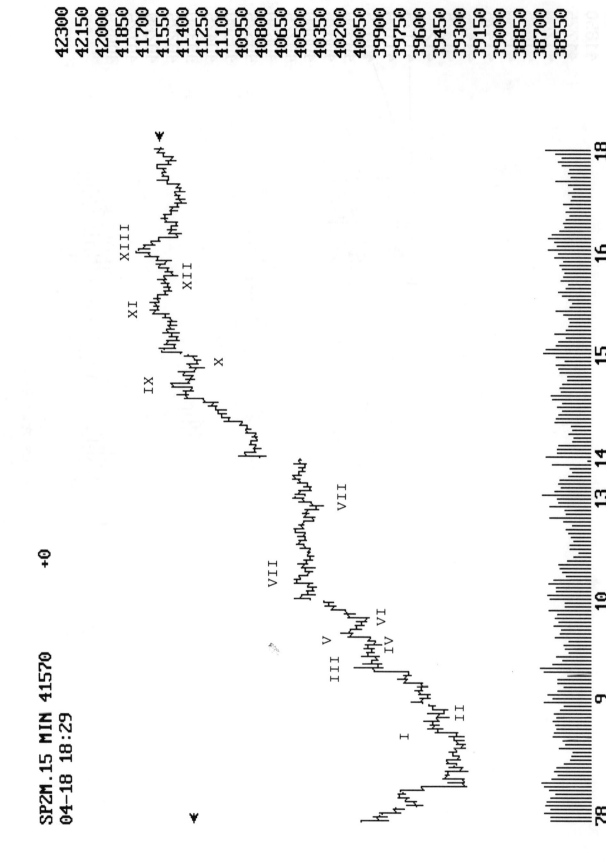

SP2M.15 MIN 41570   +0
04-18 18:29

42300
42150
42000
41850
41700
41550
41400
41250
41100
40950
40800
40650
40500
40350
40200
40050
39900
39750
39600
39450
39300
39150
39000
38850
38700
38550

Illustration 9-23

126

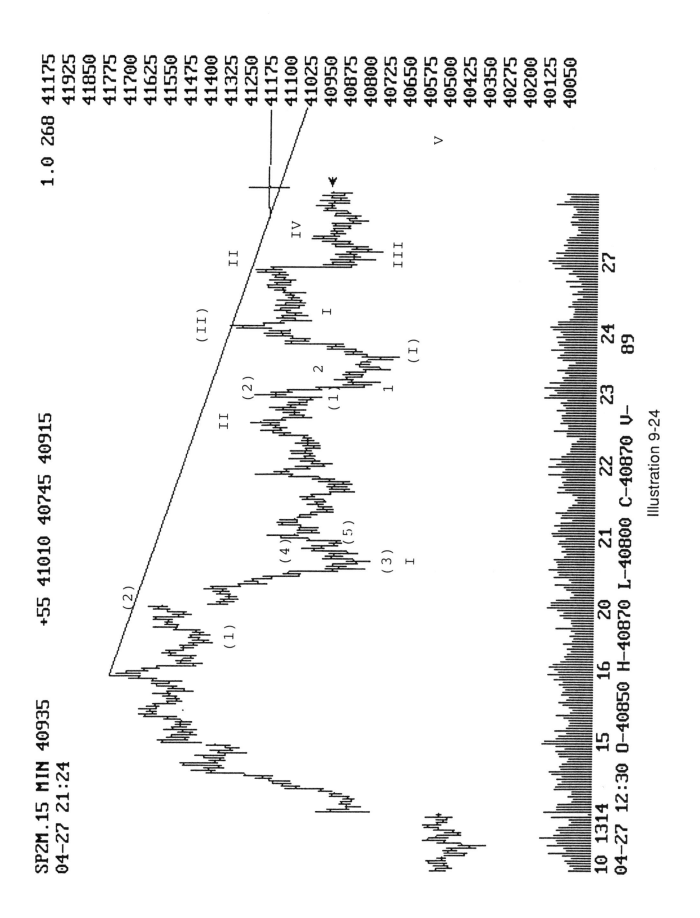

Illustration 9-24

127

Illustration 9-25

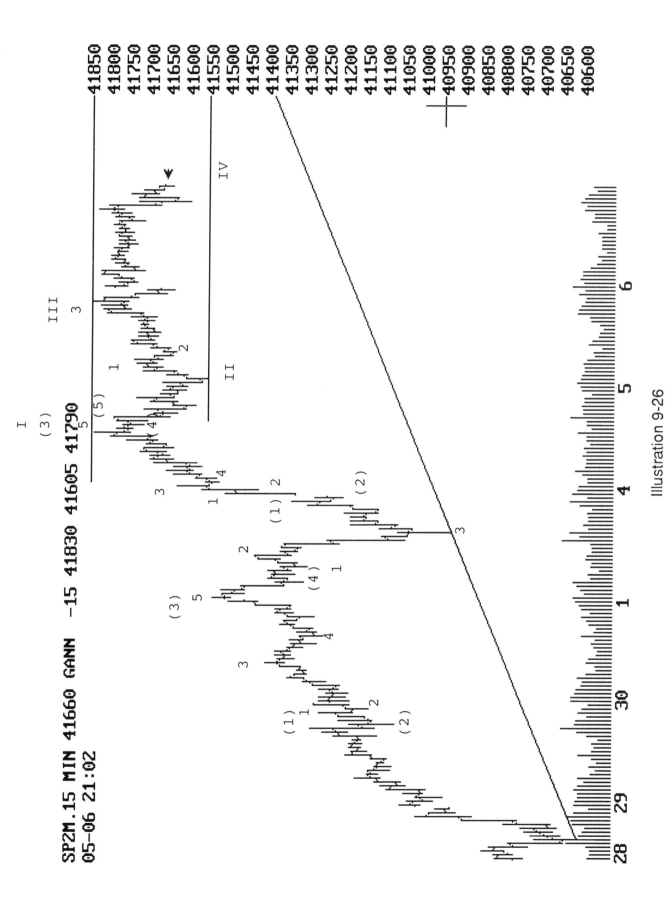

SP2M.15 MIN 41660 GANN -15 41830 41605 41790
05-06 21:02

Illustration 9-26

129

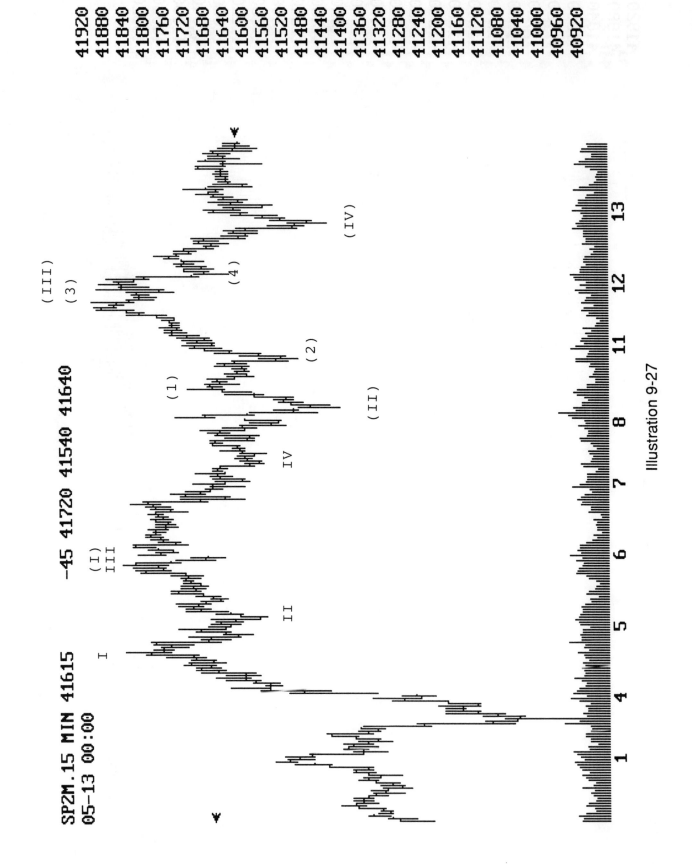

Illustration 9-27

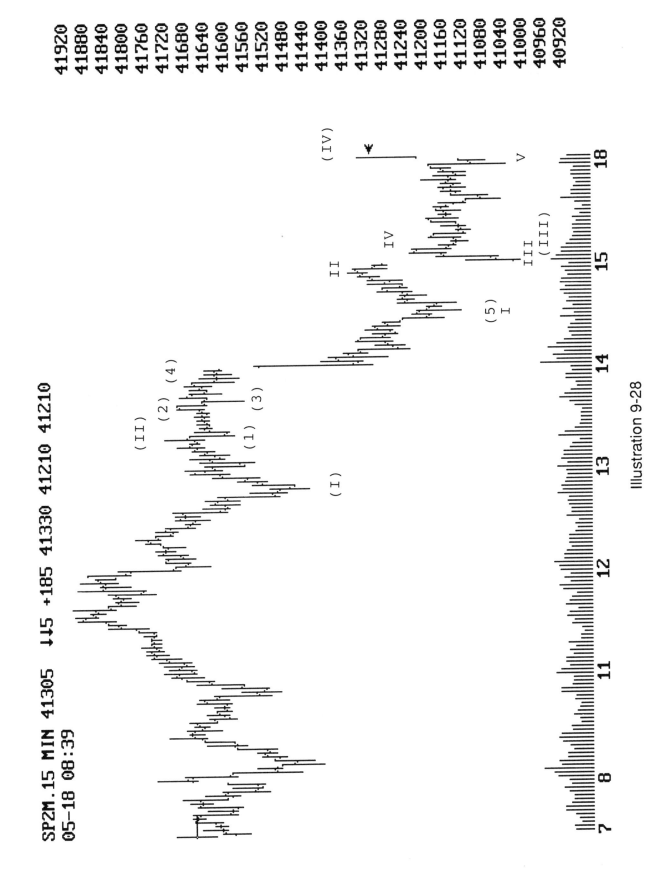

Illustration 9-28

131

FIBONACCI RATIOS

Fibonacci ratios are named after a 17th Century mathematician who discovered that dividing certain odd numbers resulted in a ratio of .618. This ratio is also known as the Golden ratio. Here is how Fibonacci came up with the Golden ratio. Three is divided by five, then three is added to five, and five is then divided by eight. Five is then added to eight and the resulting number thirteen divides eight. This pattern continues, each time adding the previous number to the current number and the new number dividing the previous number. Below are some examples.

$$3/5 \quad = .600$$
$$5/8 \quad = .625$$
$$8/13 \quad = .615$$
$$13/21 \quad = .619$$

. . . and so on.

The average of these ratios is .618. Besides the Golden ratio number as a popular support or resistance point, there are derivatives that are equally popular. These derivatives are as follows: .26, .38, .50, .618, .73, .85. The idea is that the markets retrace to one of these ratios before continuing their trend. Of the above ratios, the most popular ones are the 50% retracement and the 62% retracement; however, in my research I have found the 73% retracement to be as powerful if not more powerful than either of the previous two ratios. Following are illustrations of how to calculate the ratios using the charts.

Use the range between a major support and a resistance price to calculate the ratios. In illustration 10-1, the Eurodollars market is used for illustrating a proper way of calculating the potential Fibonacci support prices. The range between a key support and resistance price is calculated, and then this range is multiplied by the Fibonacci ratios. In illustration 10-1, a major support and a major resistance price are labeled. The next step is to use this range to calculate the possible percentage of retracement. Support is at $95.09 and Resistance is at $97.01, and by subtracting $95.09 from $97.01 we get a range of $1.92. At this point we will calculate several different Fibonacci ratios:

EURODOLLAR WEEKLY CHART

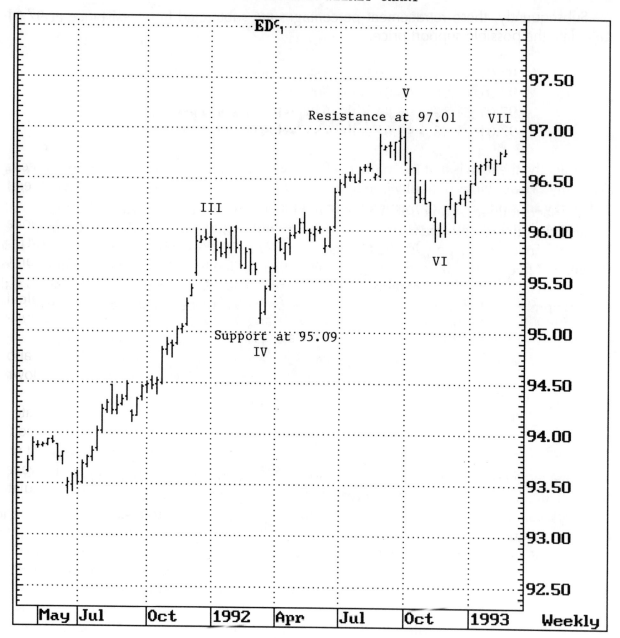

Illustration 10-1

$$1.92 \times .38 = .72$$
$$1.92 \times .50 = .96$$
$$1.92 \times .61 = 1.17$$
$$1.92 \times .73 = 1.40$$

Subsequently, these retracement percentages are subtracted from resistance at 97.01 to calculate the possible support price.

$$97.01 - .72 = 96.29 \text{ is the 38\% retracement price.}$$
$$97.01 - .96 = 96.05 \text{ is the 50\% retracement price.}$$
$$97.01 - 1.17 = 95.84 \text{ is the 61\% retracement price.}$$
$$97.01 - 1.40 = 95.61 \text{ is the 73\% retracement price.}$$

Basically, the idea is that the market will come to one of these Fibonacci support prices and then rally. The obvious difficulty is in figuring out which one of the Fibonacci ratios will end up as the key support price from which the market will rally.

You will find Symmetry Wave to be most useful in figuring out the most likely Fibonacci support price that the market will come down to. To find the most likely Fibonacci support price, we go back in time and find a previous retracement wave on the weekly Eurodollar chart (see illustration 10-1) that the current retracement wave might match in magnitude. Looking at the magnitude of the retracement wave IV that occurred March 1992, you can proceed to calculate its magnitude. The range between trend wave III and the retracement wave IV is about .98; therefore, you can subtract .98 from $97.01 (wave V) and come up with a possible Symmetry price of $96.03. This corresponds closely with the 50% retracement as calculated above. Therefore, the most likely Fibonacci support price will be $96.05. The market came down to $95.90 and then rallied.

Similar calculations can be made for a market that is in a downtrend. To illustrate the calculations for a downtrend market, the share prices of Digital Equipment will be used (see illustration 10-2). After this market made a top on November 26 at $64.50, retracement wave VI, it went down to $48.50, trend wave VII. The difference between the retracement wave VI and trend wave VII becomes the range from which Fibonacci support prices will be calculated.

$$\text{Wave VI - Wave VII} = 16.00$$

$$16.00 \times .38 = 6.08$$
$$16.00 \times .50 = 8.00$$
$$16.00 \times .61 = 9.76$$
$$16.00 \times .73 = 11.66$$

The above ratios are added to the low of wave VII, which is at $48.50 to come up with potential resistance points.

$$48.50 + 6.08 = 54.58 \text{ is the 38\% retracement.}$$
$$48.50 + 8.00 = 56.50 \text{ is the 50\% retracement.}$$
$$48.50 + 9.76 = 58.26 \text{ is the 61\% retracement.}$$
$$48.50 + 11.66 = 60.16 \text{ is the 73\% retracement.}$$

DIGITAL EQUIPMENT DAILY CHART

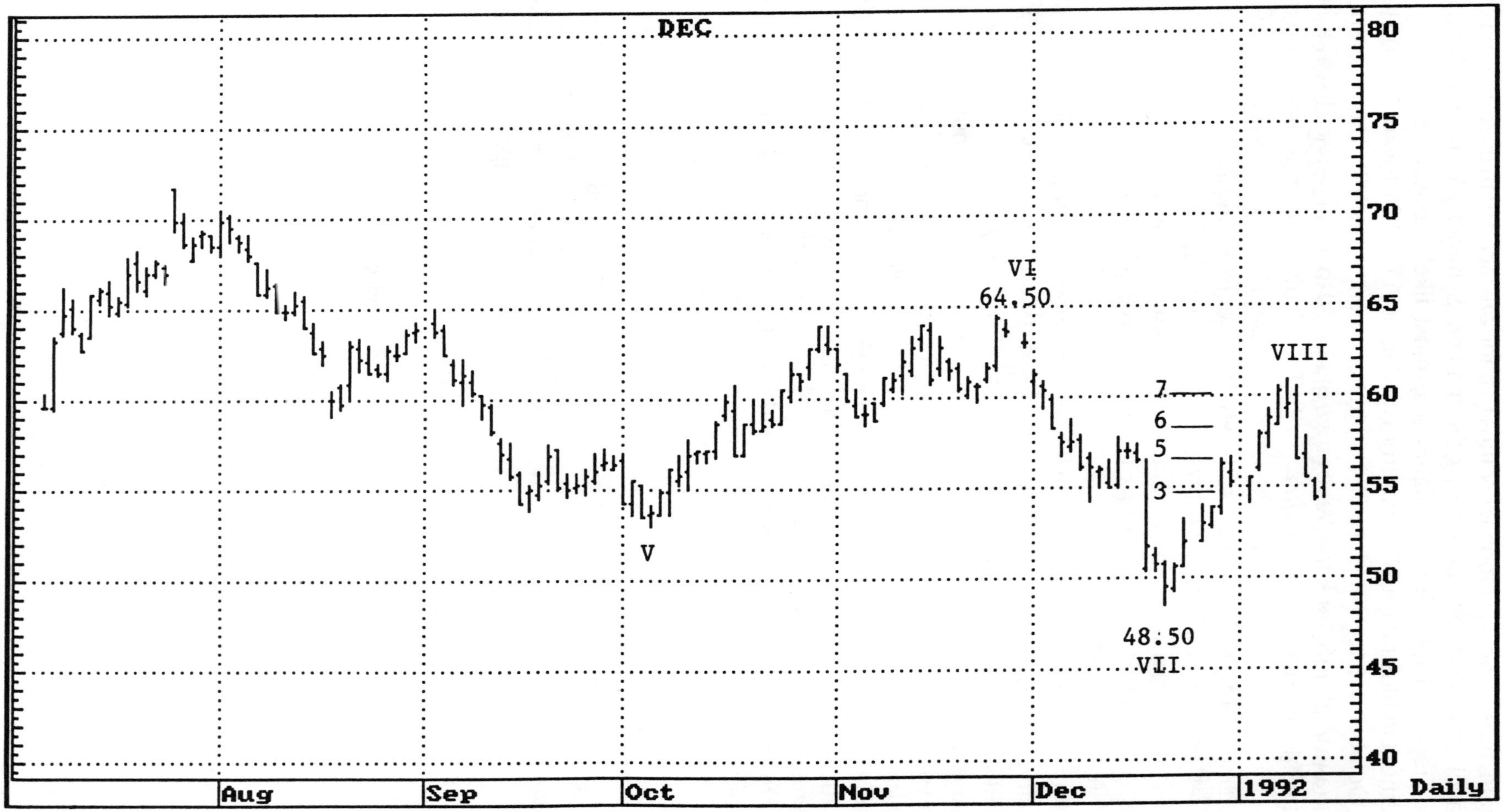

VIII

7 ———
6 ———
5 ———
3 ———

48:50
VII

VI
64.50.

DEC.

V

Daily

1992

Dec

Nov

Oct

Sep

Aug

80
75
70
65
60
55
50
45
40

Illustration 10-2

136

Again, those who use Fibonacci ratios to trade are faced with the dilemma of choosing which Fibonacci ratio is correct for entering the market. Symmetry Wave can be used to choose the proper Fibonacci ratio for calculating the most likely resistance point. The previous big retracement in illustration 10-2 was from the October 4, 1991 low of $53.00 (trend wave V), up to the October 31, 1991 high of $64.50 (retracement wave VI). The difference between wave V and wave VI is the Symmetry Wave range of $11.50 that will be used to calculate the most likely next resistance price from trend wave VII. To calculate the most likely resistance point using Symmetry Wave, add $11.50 to the December 20, 1991 low of $48.50 (wave VII), to arrive at the next most likely resistance price, that of $60.00. The closest Fibonacci ratio to the Symmetry Wave resistance price is the 73% retracement price of $60.16. This price of $60.16 is the most likely Fibonacci resistance price. The market rallied up to $61.04 and subsequently fell again. To see a clearer perspective of the Symmetry Wave count, refer to the weekly chart of Digital Equipment (illustration 10-3).

The Fibonacci ratios are similar to the ratios that W. D. Gann used. Gann's ratios were made up by dividing an entire range into one-eighths. Thus, if we divide 100 by 1/8 we get 12.5%, and its multiples are:

Gann ratios: 12.5%, 25%, 37.5%, 50%, 62.5%, 75%, and 87.5%.

FR ratios: 14.4%, 26%, 38%, 50%, 61.8%, 73.8%, and 85.6%.

Besides using Fibonacci and Gann ratios with Symmetry Wave, other tools such as Gann lines, Andrew's pitch fork lines, and trend lines can be used with Symmetry Wave.

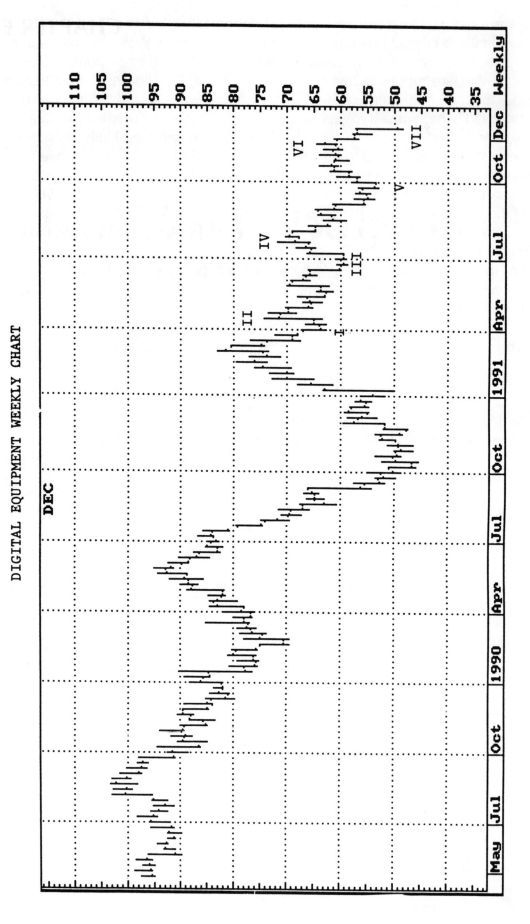

DIGITAL EQUIPMENT WEEKLY CHART

Illustration 10-3

CHAPTER ELEVEN

PSYCHOLOGY OF TRADING AND GENERAL OBSERVATIONS

In this final chapter I'll take a closer, somewhat analytical, look at some of the mind's basic behavior in relation to trading. Then I'll share some general observations about the markets.

PSYCHOLOGY

The essence of the market is obscured by hundreds of misleading price patterns and mental assumptions. In Chapter One we looked at how a person interprets three-month, six-month and longer price data in many different ways. In Chapter Two it was mentioned how, when price patterns are strung together, complex patterns are created. One of the most famous is the Elliott Wave Theory, a complex web of patterns with numerous variations which have proven not to be a great help in trading. Finally, it was shown how Symmetry Wave peels away the excess and reveals the essence of the market. That essence is the fact that markets organize themselves in symmetrical waves. To succeed you must match the same size retracement waves.

The market may get to your predicted symmetry price very rapidly or very slowly. Fact is, though, it does not matter how a market gets to the symmetry price. All assumptions and expectations need to be given up. In previous chapters, we mostly concentrated on the outer world; however, let's take a look at the "inner world" that controls how we think, speak and act in the outer world. Several years ago I created a system which I named TAAS. The system had not had a losing year since 1980. Yet, whenever I had a signal generated by TAAS, I would find reasons not to take the trade. Then, when there were no trading signals, I would find an excuse to get into the market. Invariably, TAAS trades would make money and my random trading consistently lost money. I read about different psychological theories as to why I might be doing this (fear of success, fear of failure, self-sabotage, etc.). Whatever the actual reason, there was no doubt my inner self was controlling events.

The mind is changeable. It is an instrument, and like all instruments, it can be altered. However, habits form mental grooves which the mind loves to run in, making it disinclined to change. Ego is made up of every single thought, belief, assumption and imagination. Since ego and mind are our self-identity, therein lies the difficulty of change. An individuals' beliefs and assumptions are his base; it is his security. Seeing the fallacy in one's beliefs or assumptions, and giving them up, is like jumping into the unknown, which is scary. Change is so scary it is often easier to repeat our unwanted habits, even if that means losing money year after year.

The only thing I've found for changing the mind and ego is experience. When we experience something, then we know, and assumptions are no longer necessary. By experiencing something other than what we are accustomed to, the new experience provides a new impression to replace the old one with. By repeating the new experience, gradually the old one is replaced. Now the mind has a new habit, one that is successful instead of destructive.

Our first step is to be honest enough to look at what the mind and ego have become. Second, by being honest, we get to experience whom we have become, and by gaining new experience, we have the opportunity to change. Third, by repeating new experiences we form new habits. In my own trading experience, once I realized the mistakes I was making, and saw the numerous fears I had in executing my own system, I moved from not executing any system trades to mixing system trades with my impulse trading. When I looked back over my trades, and sorted them into two groups, those generated by my system versus those generated by impulse, my system was profitable and almost all impulse trades were losers. By going through this process a number of times, gradually I found myself executing only those trades generated by my system. As I saw my trades become successful, my confidence increased. Old patterns and habits had been replaced by new, more profitable ones.

On occasion I'll do a self analysis study to better understand and improve my trading. Following is one of those studies:

Consequences of My Assumptions and Fears
During A Two-Month Trading Period

Trades Missed All-Together		Got Out Too Soon		Traded Against The Major Trend		Did Not Move The Protective Stop To Neutral	
Wheat	$500	Canadian $	- $310	D. Mark	- $400	Silver	$ - $175
Corn	500	J. Yen	- 206	Cotton	- 325	Cocoa	- 400
Soybeans	500	Euro $	- 25				
Soy Meal	500	C. Oil	- 250				
Oats	500	Nat. Gas	- 620				
Swiss Fr.	600	Sugar	- 90				
Copper	500						
Silver	500						
S&P 500	1,000						
Euro $	500						
Crude Oil	500						
Nat. Gas	1,000						
Heating Oil	500						
Heating Oil	500						
Coffee	750						
Coffee	750						
	$10,500		- 1,500		- 725		- 575

Net difference in my trading account:

$10,500 I did not earn because I did not execute on the assumption that these trades would not have worked.

$-2,800 I lost unnecessarily by trading contrarily to guidelines established for myself.

When adding the dollar amount of the trades I did not execute to the foregone profits from my mistakes, the total comes to **$13,300 in two months**. I marked each of these trades on a chart so that I could easily see what I had done. Missing out on $13,300 in two months was a big disappointment, but it helped me gain confidence in Symmetry Wave and start to take all the trades it generated.

I realized by *repeating* a positive action (i.e. - adhering to personal guidelines for successful trading) enough times, I could replace my old habits with new.

Trading the markets will bring the weaknesses that are hidden within each one of us to the forefront. This is a significant benefit of trading. It forces a trader to give up assumptions and to become practical. Maintaining a daily journal detailing which assumption kept you from executing an aspect of a trading system will help you give up negative or erroneous assumptions and become more practical. To succeed, you often have to give up (or change) many assumptions, and learn to just practically apply your knowledge of trading.

STRESS

External control can be defined as the self-imposed conditions or parameters a person sets for trading the markets. Some external controls are: when to enter the market, how much to risk, when to take a profit, and how many contracts to buy or sell for each trade. By contrast, internal control is how we react emotionally and intellectually to the unknowns associated with the market. Questions that are unknown in trading include these:

1. Will the system I am following be successful in the next few months?
2. Should I stay with this system after four losing trades?
3. Corn looks like a buy, but soybeans look like a sell. Since they tend to move in conjunction, which way should I trade?
4. Should I wait a little longer and thereby miss a profitable trade, or jump in now?
5. Should I use a tight stop or wide stop?
6. Should I take my $400 profit now, or do I wait longer and shoot for a $1,000 profit?

Obviously, for each of these questions (and countless others raised daily when trading) there is no one correct answer. Regardless of the choice made, the outcome of that specific decision is unknown. Stress arises when one has to make a decision between two or more choices and the outcome of either choice is unknown; or, having made a decision, stress arises when you have no control over the outcome. Since each one of the above questions requires a decision, and since the decision is based on unknown outcomes, a trader continuously faces stress. Stress is a natural defensive reaction. Science tells us when under stress there are specific biochemical reactions, such as a release of hormones, which as a defensive measure of the body causes one to react. Besides the biochemical component of stress, there is the mental component, worry.

Worry involves concern about one's decision and its consequences. Every time a decision relating to trading has to be made, there is a subsequent tendency to worry about the unknown consequences. Without a doubt, worry impairs analytical thinking. This means we give up being practical and become assumptive. Also, the amount of worry associated with trading the market substantially increases stress. Then, to abate the constant mental duress caused by worry, a person tends to make any decision that will appease stress. And even a decision not to do substantially increases stress. Then, to abate the constant mental duress caused by worry, a person tends to make any decision that will appease stress. And even a decision not to do anything still has unknown consequences and carries with it potential stress. Why? Because a missed opportunity to make $1,500 can also be quite stressful.

I have found that many traders mirror the market. This is most likely due to the need to appease worry and stress. If your most recent trade was stopped out prematurely due to a tight stop, the worry that on the next trade the same thing will happen often leads to the use of a wider stop. Often the reverse also happens, whereby a person loses a big chunk of money because of an excessively wide stop and is then afraid to use a wide stop for the next trade. The important point is not whether to use a wide or tight stop, but to have the proper internal control so that the stress level does not rule or cloud decision-making. It is the reaction to worry and stress that causes one to fail more than anything else in trading. When you add "greed" into the mix, with its mistaken emphasis on speed over consistency and patience, it's no wonder there is such a high failure rate among traders.

Psychologists are finding that incentive impairs human performance by focusing attention on the outcome (in this case, to make money or to preserve money) rather than the solution. The solution for us as traders lies more on internal control rather than external control. Internal control is achieved by recognizing the influence of worry, greed, stress and assumptions; and to adopt a set of new attitudes towards the markets so that the ever-changing market conditions do not overpower you as a trader. The easiest way to change is to repeat the right action over and over again until old habits and impressions are replaced by new.

It is logical to conclude that internal control and external control are intertwined. If some degree of internal control is not achieved, then under the influence of stress a person is likely *not* to follow his predetermined set of external controls (i.e. - entry price and exit price). On the other hand, if one does not have a set of *predetermined* external controls, then a person *continually* has to make a stressful decision.

By following the Symmetry Wave trading rules, executing each aspect of the method repeatedly and consistently, new successful experiences will force out the old habits of worry, stress and incorrect assumptions.

A technique that helps in reinforcing and motivating a trader to execute his trades is visualization. Visualization is really just remembering. Remember why you chose a specific size protective stop or profit target, remember why you chose early entry over late entry and remember how it feels to win over a period of time. Remembrance or visualization motivates, but the real change happens only by executing the right habits. By *experiencing* the impression and feelings, new habits replace the old ones.

GENERAL OBSERVATIONS

1. Regardless of the trading system used, approximately 30% of winning trades move extensively in one's favor immediately. What this means is that the best trades often do not give a second chance to execute them. You must put all your entry orders in before the market reaches the entry price.

2. Experts, whether we talk about newspapers, brokers, advisors or some other type of guru, are not necessarily better than the layman. They are only more knowledgeable in the mechanics of how things work. Therefore, if you have studied Symmetry Wave (which takes the randomness out of the markets, and organizes them) then you could become a greater expert.

3.	If you acquire too many positions in relation to your comfort level, then the increased level of stress will often cause you to overlook or bypass several key aspects of your trading program, including the entry guidelines and protective stops.

4.	I have tested many systems with up to 900 variations of profit targets and protective stops. The most profitable combination could earn $60,000 or more, while the worst combination might lose $60,000 or more. Avoid curve-fit mechanical systems like these whose parameters can be manipulated. You will find Symmetry Wave to be far superior, as it is an organizational method that uncovers balance points. It is not a rigid mechanical system, but rather an intelligent, adaptive one.

5.	Markets change their patterns about every six months to a year. This material shifting in behavior often wreaks havoc on mechanical systems.

6.	Trading frequently is not necessarily more profitable. People who trade less often tend to be more successful. A broker friend told me he had one client wait a year before putting on a position. That market was at historical highs, then dropped rapidly. The man made over $200,000 and stopped trading.

7.	Weekly charts give an excellent overall perspective of a given trend.

8.	Most major trends last six months or longer. You can and should take advantage of the sizable corrections which occur within that time period.

9.	It is counterproductive to day-trade more than one market.

10.	Avoid the market noise (small price fluctuations) and concentrate on the waves that are at least "one times the ATR." Also, try not to pay attention to what you do not need. More information tends to create confusion.

11.	After a drawdown, the average recovery period for mutual funds is about 27 months. Many futures funds also experience long recovery periods after a drawdown.

12.	Five-minute bar charts yield the worst profit-to-loss ratio. Weekly charts yield the highest profit-to-loss ratio.

13.	Try to give up past assumptions about the markets. Symmetry Wave fixes your focus, instead, on a unique aspect of analysis (the matching of retracement waves) not on where and how markets close, or volatility or price patterns. As an example of acting on different assumptions with Symmetry Wave, I have, on occasion, entered markets when they retraced three times the ATR in one day, with the market closing at its low of the day. The next day the market almost inevitably starts to rally.

14.	Avoid basing your next trading decision on what may have happened on your previous trade. If you base trading decisions on what has happened in the past, then you will be constantly adjusting the entry method, protective stops and profit targets. There is no ideal.

15. Many traders take a profit at their profit target, then, when they see they could have made a greater profit, curse themselves. That's a terrible way to live. With a negative outlook, even if you are a winner, you make yourself feel like a loser.

16. By testing many computerized systems, I've found that even with a high accuracy trading system, there are many strings of five to six losses.

17. With Symmetry Wave, even when trading similar markets such as Deutsche Mark and Swiss Franc, or Exxon and Mobil, pay attention to each individual market's unique signals. Often it happens that the Deutsche Mark may reach its symmetry price, while the Swiss Franc may not.

18. Focus on results, not from just a few hours or days, but from several months to a year.

19. The assumptive nature of the mind and ego must be considered so that unwanted fear can be avoided.

20. Fear of losing tends to keep traders out of the markets, while fear of missing a trade causes traders to jump into a market before it is time to do so.

21. For most people it is a false assumption to believe that they can do better by watching the markets throughout the day.

22. The vast majority of systems are curve-fit to past data. These systems only work for short periods of time, usually lasting four to twelve months before entering into a cycle when they do not work for four to twelve months.

23. Do not adjust a method that is already working, and make sure any adjustment is paper traded first.

24. The formula for success in trading is 50% self-analysis, 25% money management and 25% a good system.

25. If your account is overloaded with trades, the additional stress may cause you to not follow your own parameters.

26. A peculiar phenomenon about the markets is that time appears to be condensed. The markets have great leverage and can generate phenomenal profits. This creates the illusion that what should be achieved in six months, a year, or even several years is expected to be achieved not only in a week, but every week.

27. Three areas within which the mind will create assumptions are entry, exit and protective stop placement. Set your parameters in advance, and make the ability to follow your parameters your enjoyment.

28. Keep a daily diary of trades, recording the thoughts or beliefs that made you follow (or *not* follow) your entry, protective stop and profit target guidelines.

29. Fills, when trading through a discount broker, are not satisfactory. In addition, fills at New York exchanges are consistently worse than with the Chicago exchanges.

30. Consistency in repeating a positive experience is the key to forming new habits and to success. It is also the best way to build confidence and to understand the intricacies of Symmetry Wave trading.

For more information on additional Symmetry Wave products and services, Michael Gur can be contacted at this address:

Michael Gur
Symmetry Wave Trading
1705 14th Street, #277
Boulder, CO 80302

Phone: 303-449-4601 • 303-595-5896
